Who is My Father?

Apostle Bill Amor

Who is My Father?
written by Bill Amor
1st Edition © 2025 by Bill Amor
ISBN: 979-8-9995696-1-5

CONTENTS

CONTENTS

CONTENTS

"Who Is My Father?" is indeed a fitting and thought-provoking title for this book and the information it provides. It encapsulates the central theme of exploring the spiritual relationship between humanity and God as the ultimate Father, while also addressing the biblical teachings about earthly authority, truth, and correction. This title invites readers to reflect on their own understanding of divine authority, their spiritual identity, and how they align with Gods truth versus worldly lies.

The title resonates deeply with the verses discussed—John 3:16, Matthew 23:9, and Proverbs 15:5—as it raises questions about recognizing God as the ultimate Father in heaven (Matthew 23:9), understanding His love and sacrifice through Jesus Christ (John 3:16), and responding wisely to instruction or correction (Proverbs 15:5). It also opens up broader discussions about spiritual parentage, moral alignment (truth vs. lies), and personal accountability under divine guidance.

"Who Is My Father?", will appeal to readers seeking clarity on their spiritual journey, encouraging them to delve into scripture for answers about their relationship with God and their role as children of truth rather than children of lies.

Summary for "Who is My Father?" by Apostle Bill Amor

In *"Who is My Father?"*, Apostle Bill Amor delves deeply into the spiritual and biblical understanding of God as the ultimate Father, drawing from key scriptures such as John 3:16, Matthew 23:9, and Proverbs 15:5. This thought-provoking book explores the profound relationship between humanity and God, emphasizing His role as the one true Father in heaven. Through careful analysis of scripture, Amor contrasts the lives of those who live as "Children of the Truth" with those who follow lies, illustrating how our response to divine instruction shapes our spiritual identity.

The book begins with an exploration of John 3:16, highlighting God's immense love for humanity and His gift of eternal life through Jesus Christ. Amor explains that accepting this truth makes believers children of God—aligned with truth and righteousness. He then examines Matthew 23:9, where Jesus instructs His followers not to call anyone on earth their father in a spiritual sense, pointing instead to God as the ultimate authority and source of guidance. This teaching challenges readers to evaluate their loyalties and recognize God's sovereignty over all earthly relationships.

Amor also draws connections to Proverbs 15:5, which contrasts the attitudes of fools who reject correction with wise individuals who embrace reproof. He uses this verse to illustrate how humility and a willingness to learn are hallmarks of those who live as children of truth under God's fatherly care. By rejecting arrogance and embracing divine discipline, believers grow in wisdom and align themselves more closely with God's will.

Throughout *"Who is My Father?"*, Apostle Bill Amor weaves together these scriptural insights to provide a compelling narrative about identity, authority, and spiritual growth. The book challenges readers to reflect on their relationship with God as their heavenly Father while encouraging them to reject falsehoods and embrace the transformative power of truth. With its rich biblical foundation and practical applications, this work serves as both a guide and an inspiration for anyone seeking a deeper connection with their Creator.

John 3:16 and Related Verses in KJV and AMP

John 3:16 (KJV):
"For God so loved the world, that he gave his only begotten Son, that whosoever believeth in him should not perish, but have everlasting life."

John 3:16 (AMP):
"For God so [greatly] loved and dearly prized the world, that He [even] gave His [One and] only begotten Son, so that whoever believes and trusts in Him [as Savior] shall not perish, but have eternal life."

Matthew 23:9 (KJV):
"And call no man your father upon the earth: for one is your Father, which is in heaven."

Matthew 23:9 (AMP):
"Do not call anyone on earth [who guides you spiritually] your father; for One is your Father, He who is in heaven."

Proverbs 15:5 (KJV):
"A fool despiseth his father's instruction: but he that regardeth reproof is prudent."

Proverbs 15:5 (AMP):
"A [flippant, arrogant] fool rejects his father's instruction and correction, but he who [is willing to learn and] regards and keeps in mind a reprimand acquires good sense."

Similarities Between Children of the Lie/Truth and Proverbs 15:5

The concept of "Children of the lie" versus "Children of the truth" aligns with Proverbs 15:5 through their attitudes toward instruction and correction. In Proverbs 15:5, a fool despises his father's guidance while a wise person values reproof. Similarly, those who follow lies reject divine truth and correction from God—their heavenly Father—while those who embrace truth are open to God's discipline.

Both passages emphasize a relationship with authority figures—whether earthly or divine. Matthew 23:9 reminds believers to recognize God as their ultimate Father. This parallels Proverbs' teaching about respecting paternal wisdom. Rejecting God's truth or earthly parental guidance reflects arrogance or foolishness akin to being "children of the lie." Conversely, accepting correction demonstrates humility and wisdom characteristic of "children of the truth."

Furthermore, John 3:16 highlights God's love as foundational for salvation. Those who believe in Christ become children of God (truth), aligning with His will. Rejecting this gift places individuals among those who live by lies—denying God's authority as their Father.

In essence, all three verses underscore submission to rightful authority—God's ultimate sovereignty—and how one's response to instruction determines alignment with truth or lies.

1. The Eternal Father: Understanding John 3:16

2. God's Love for Humanity: A Gift Beyond Measure

3. Becoming Children of God: Accepting the Truth

4. The Role of Jesus Christ in Revealing the Father

5. Matthew 23:9 and the Call to Recognize God as Father

6. Earthly Fathers vs. The Heavenly Father: A Biblical Perspective

7. Spiritual Authority and God's Sovereignty Over All Relationships

8. Proverbs 15:5: Wisdom in Embracing Correction

9. Fools and the Rejection of Instruction: Lessons from

Proverbs

Chapter 1: The Eternal Father: Understanding John 3:16

John 3:16 is one of the most well-known and beloved verses in the Bible. It reads, "For God so loved the world that He gave His only begotten Son, that whoever believes in Him should not perish but have everlasting life." This single verse encapsulates the essence of God's love for humanity and His role as our eternal Father. In this chapter, we will delve deeply into the profound truths contained within this scripture, exploring its implications for our understanding of God as the ultimate Father and what it means to live as His children.

The Father's Love for Humanity

At the heart of John 3:16 lies an extraordinary declaration of love. The verse begins with "For God so loved the world," emphasizing the depth and scope of God's affection for all people. Unlike human love, which can be conditional or limited, God's love is infinite and unchanging. It extends to every individual, regardless of their background, sins, or shortcomings. This universal love underscores God's identity as a Father who desires a relationship with each of His children.

The Greek word used for "love" in this verse is *agape*, which signifies a selfless, sacrificial love that seeks the best for others without expecting anything in return. This type of love is central to God's nature and serves as the foundation for His actions toward humanity. As our eternal Father, God demonstrates *agape* by providing us with everything we need—not just physically but spiritually as well.

The Gift of Jesus Christ

The second part of John 3:16 reveals how God expressed His love: "He gave His only begotten Son." This act of giving was not merely a gesture; it was a profound sacrifice. By sending Jesus Christ into the world, God provided a way for humanity to be reconciled to Him. Jesus' life, death, and resurrection are the ultimate expressions of God's fatherly care and commitment to our well-being.

The term "only begotten" (Greek: *monogenes*) highlights Jesus' unique relationship with the Father. While all believers are considered children of God through faith (Galatians 3:26), Jesus holds a special status as the eternal Son who shares in the divine nature. This distinction underscores the magnitude of God's gift—He did not spare even His own Son to secure our salvation (Romans 8:32).

By giving Jesus, God opened the door for us to become part of His family. Through faith in Christ, we are adopted as sons and daughters (Ephesians 1:5). This adoption is not merely symbolic; it is a transformative reality that changes our spiritual identity and aligns us with God's truth and righteousness.

Eternal Life Through Faith

The latter half of John 3:16 focuses on the promise attached to belief in Jesus: "that whoever believes in Him should not perish but have everlasting life." Here, we see two contrasting outcomes—perishing versus eternal life—and a clear path to avoid destruction through faith.

To "believe" in Jesus means more than intellectual assent; it involves trusting Him completely as Lord and Savior. This faith connects us to God as our Father and secures our place in His family forever. Eternal life is not just about living forever; it is about experiencing an unbroken relationship with God—a life filled with purpose, joy, and peace that begins now and continues into eternity.

As children of God, we are called to live in light of this promise. Our lives should reflect gratitude for what He has done and a commitment to follow His ways. By embracing our identity as His children, we align ourselves with truth and reject the lies that seek to pull us away from Him.

Living as Children of Truth

John 3:16 challenges us to consider how we respond to God's love and invitation. Do we accept Him as our eternal Father or turn away in pursuit of worldly desires? Those who choose to believe become "children of truth," walking in alignment with God's will and reflecting His character in their daily lives.

Living as children of truth requires humility—a willingness to acknowledge our need for correction and guidance from our heavenly Father (Proverbs 15:5). It also involves rejecting falsehoods that contradict Scripture and standing firm in faith despite opposition or temptation.

In practical terms, this means prioritizing our relationship with God above all else. It means seeking Him through prayer, studying His Word diligently, and obeying His commands out of love rather than obligation. As we grow closer to Him, we begin to see ourselves—and others—through His eyes.

Conclusion

John 3:16 offers a powerful glimpse into God's heart as our eternal Father. It reveals a love so profound that He was willing to sacrifice everything for us—a love that invites us into an everlasting relationship with Him through faith in Jesus Christ.

As you reflect on this verse, consider what it means for your own life. Have you embraced your identity as a child of God? Are you living in alignment with His truth? Remember that being part of God's family is both a privilege and a responsibility—one that calls us to live out His love every day.

By understanding John 3:16 more deeply, we can begin to grasp the enormity of God's fatherly care and respond by walking faithfully as His beloved children.

Chapter 2: God's Love for Humanity: A Gift Beyond Measure

In Chapter 2 of *Who is My Father?*, Apostle Bill Amor delves deeply into the profound and immeasurable love that God has for humanity. This chapter builds upon the foundational truth found in John 3:16, one of the most well-known and cherished verses in the Bible: "For God so loved the world that He gave His only begotten Son, that whoever believes in Him should not perish but have everlasting life." Through this verse, Amor invites readers to reflect on the depth of God's love and its implications for our spiritual identity and eternal destiny.

The Nature of God's Love

God's love is unique in its nature—it is unconditional, sacrificial, and eternal. Unlike human love, which can often be conditional or limited by circumstances, God's love transcends all boundaries. It is a love that does not depend on our worthiness or actions but is freely given to all. As Apostle Paul writes in Romans 5:8, "But God demonstrates His own love toward us, in that while we were still sinners, Christ died for us." This selfless act underscores the magnitude of God's love—a love so great that it compelled Him to sacrifice His only Son for the redemption of humanity.

Amor emphasizes that understanding this divine love requires humility and faith. It is not something we can fully comprehend with our finite minds but must accept as a gift beyond measure. This acceptance transforms our relationship with God, allowing us to see Him not just as a distant deity but as a loving Father who desires an intimate relationship with His children.

The Gift of Jesus Christ

Central to God's expression of love is the gift of Jesus Christ. In sending His Son into the world, God provided a way for humanity to be reconciled to Him. Jesus' life, death, and resurrection are the ultimate demonstration of God's commitment to saving us from sin and granting us eternal life. As Amor explains, this gift is not something we can earn through good works or religious rituals; it is a free gift offered to all who believe in Jesus as their Savior.

John 3:16 highlights two key aspects of this gift: its universality and its exclusivity. On one hand, God's love extends to "the world," encompassing every person regardless of race, nationality, or background. On the other hand, salvation is available only to those who believe in Jesus Christ. This duality challenges readers to consider their own response to God's offer of grace—will they accept it and live as children of truth or reject it and remain separated from their Heavenly Father?

Living as Recipients of Divine Love

Receiving God's love is not merely an intellectual acknowledgment; it requires a transformation of heart and mind. Amor encourages readers to reflect on how this divine love should shape their lives. As recipients of such an extraordinary gift, believers are called to live in gratitude and obedience to God's will. This includes loving others as God has loved us (John 13:34-35) and sharing the message of salvation with those who have yet to experience His grace.

Furthermore, living as recipients of divine love means trusting in God's plan even when circumstances seem difficult or uncertain. Romans 8:28 reminds us that "all things work together for good to those who love God." This assurance allows believers to face life's challenges with confidence, knowing that their Heavenly Father is always working for their ultimate good.

Contrasting Divine Love with Worldly Love

Amor also contrasts God's perfect love with the flawed expressions of love often seen in the world. While worldly love can be self-serving or fleeting, divine love is selfless and enduring. Proverbs 15:5 serves as a reminder that true wisdom comes from embracing correction and guidance from our Heavenly Father—a reflection of His deep care for us.

This contrast highlights the importance of aligning our understanding of love with biblical truth rather than cultural norms or personal preferences. By doing so, we can better appreciate the depth of God's affection for us and strive to emulate His example in our relationships with others.

Conclusion: A Call to Respond

In closing this chapter, Amor issues a heartfelt call for readers to respond to God's incredible gift of love. He urges them not only to accept this gift through faith in Jesus Christ but also to let it transform every aspect of their lives. By doing so, they can experience the fullness of what it means to be children of God—loved unconditionally by their Heavenly Father and empowered by His Spirit to walk in truth and righteousness.

God's love for humanity truly is a gift beyond measure—one that offers hope, purpose, and eternal life through Jesus Christ. As Amor eloquently states at the end of this chapter: "To know God's love is not merely an emotional experience; it is an invitation into a relationship that changes everything."

Chapter 3: Becoming Children of God: Accepting the Truth

The journey to becoming children of God begins with a profound and personal decision: accepting the truth revealed through Jesus Christ. This chapter delves into the transformative process of embracing God's truth, as outlined in scripture, and explores how this acceptance shapes our spiritual identity and relationship with Him as our Father.

Understanding the Foundation: John 3:16

John 3:16 serves as the cornerstone for understanding what it means to become a child of God. The verse states:

"For God so loved the world that He gave His one and only Son, that whoever believes in Him shall not perish but have eternal life."

This passage reveals two critical truths about God's nature and His plan for humanity. First, it emphasizes God's immense love for all people—a love so great that He was willing to sacrifice His only Son, Jesus Christ, to redeem us from sin. Second, it highlights the pathway to becoming a child of God: belief in Jesus Christ as Lord and Savior.

To accept this truth is to acknowledge both our need for salvation and God's provision of grace through Jesus. It requires humility to admit our imperfections and faith to trust in God's promise of eternal life.

The Role of Faith in Becoming Children of God

Faith is central to our adoption into God's family. In Galatians 3:26, Paul writes:

"So in Christ Jesus you are all children of God through faith."

This verse underscores that our status as God's children is not based on works or heritage but on faith in Jesus Christ. By placing our trust in Him, we are spiritually reborn into a new identity—one that aligns us with truth and righteousness.

Jesus Himself spoke about this transformation when He told Nicodemus, "Very truly I tell you, no one can see the kingdom of God unless they are born again" (John 3:3). This "new birth" is a spiritual awakening that occurs when we accept the truth of who Jesus is and what He has done for us.

Contrasting Truth with Lies

In becoming children of God, we must also reject falsehoods that contradict His truth. The Bible frequently contrasts those who live by truth with those who follow lies. For example, John 8:44 describes Satan as "the father of lies," highlighting his role in leading people away from God.

As children of God, we are called to discern between truth and deception by grounding ourselves in scripture. Psalm

119:105 declares:

"Your word is a lamp for my feet, a light on my path."

By studying God's Word and applying its principles to our lives, we can navigate the challenges of a world filled with conflicting messages and remain steadfast in our commitment to truth.

Living as Children of Truth

Accepting the truth is not merely an intellectual exercise; it involves a complete transformation of how we live. Ephesians 5:8-9 encourages believers:

"For you were once darkness, but now you are light in the Lord. Live as children of light (for the fruit of the light consists in all goodness, righteousness and truth)."

Living as children of light means reflecting God's character through our actions. It involves demonstrating love, kindness, integrity, and humility—qualities that set us apart as His representatives on earth.

Moreover, living as children of truth requires obedience to God's commands. In John 14:15, Jesus said:

"If you love me, keep my commands."

Obedience is not about earning God's favor but about expressing gratitude for His grace and aligning ourselves with His will.

The Assurance of Our Identity

One of the most comforting aspects of becoming a child of God is the assurance it brings. Romans 8:16-17 affirms:

"The Spirit himself testifies with our spirit that we are God's children. Now if we are children, then we are heirs—heirs of God and co-heirs with Christ."

This passage reminds us that our identity as God's children is secure because it is sealed by the Holy Spirit. As heirs alongside Christ, we have access to all the blessings promised by our Heavenly Father—including eternal life.

Conclusion

Becoming a child of God begins with accepting the truth revealed through Jesus Christ. It involves acknowledging His love and sacrifice, placing our faith in Him for salvation, rejecting falsehoods that lead us astray, living according to His Word, and embracing our new identity as members of His family.

This transformation is not something we achieve on our own; it is made possible by God's grace working within us. As Philippians 2:13 reminds us:

"For it is God who works in you to will and to act in order to fulfill his good purpose."

By accepting this truth wholeheartedly—and allowing it to shape every aspect of our lives—we can experience the fullness of what it means to be called "children of God."

Chapter 4: The Role of Jesus Christ in Revealing the Father

The role of Jesus Christ in revealing God as the Father is one of the most profound and central themes in Christian theology. Throughout the New Testament, Jesus consistently emphasizes His unique relationship with God and His mission to make the Father known to humanity. This chapter explores how Jesus serves as the ultimate revelation of God's character, love, and authority, providing believers with a clear understanding of what it means to know and relate to God as their Heavenly Father.

1. Jesus as the Image of the Invisible God

The Apostle Paul writes in Colossians 1:15 that Jesus is "the image of the invisible God." This statement underscores that Jesus embodies the fullness of God's nature in human form. Through His life, teachings, and actions, Jesus provides a tangible representation of who God is. Unlike any prophet or teacher before Him, Jesus does not merely speak about God—He reveals Him directly. As John 14:9 records, Jesus tells Philip, "Anyone who has seen me has seen the Father." This declaration affirms that knowing Jesus is synonymous with knowing God.

By becoming incarnate, Jesus bridges the gap between humanity and divinity. He allows us to see God's attributes— His love, mercy, justice, and holiness—manifested in ways we can understand and relate to. In this sense, Jesus serves as both a mirror reflecting God's character and a window through which we can glimpse His divine nature.

2. The Father's Love Demonstrated Through Christ

One of the most significant ways Jesus reveals the Father is by demonstrating His immense love for humanity. John 3:16 encapsulates this truth: "For God so loved the world that He gave His one and only Son." The sacrificial death of Jesus on the cross is not only an act of redemption but also a profound expression of God's fatherly love.

Through His ministry on earth, Jesus consistently points people to this love. He heals the sick (Matthew 8:16-17), forgives sins (Luke 7:48), and welcomes outcasts (Luke 19:10), showing that God's love extends to all people regardless of their status or past mistakes. These actions reveal a compassionate Father who desires reconciliation with His children.

Moreover, in parables such as "The Prodigal Son" (Luke 15:11-32), Jesus illustrates God's readiness to forgive and restore those who turn back to Him. The father in this story represents God's boundless grace—a theme central to understanding our relationship with Him.

3. Jesus as Mediator Between Humanity and the Father

Another critical aspect of Christ's role is His function as a mediator between humanity and God. In John 14:6, Jesus declares, "I am the way and the truth and the life. No one comes to the Father except through me." This statement highlights that access to God as our Father is made possible only through faith in Christ.

As both fully divine and fully human, Jesus uniquely qualifies to bridge this divide caused by sin (1 Timothy 2:5). By taking upon Himself the punishment for sin through His death on the cross (Isaiah 53:5), He removes every barrier separating us from God's presence. Consequently, believers are adopted into God's family (Romans 8:15) and can approach Him with confidence as their loving Father.

4. Teaching About Prayer and Relationship With the Father

Jesus not only reveals who God is but also teaches how we should relate to Him as our Heavenly Father. In Matthew 6:9-13—the Lord's Prayer—Jesus instructs His disciples to address God as "Our Father," emphasizing intimacy while acknowledging His holiness ("hallowed be Your name"). This prayer reflects a balance between reverence for God's majesty and trust in His personal care.

Furthermore, throughout His ministry, Jesus models dependence on and communion with the Father through prayer (Mark 1:35; Luke 5:16). By doing so, He demonstrates that an ongoing relationship with God requires humility, faithfulness, and intentional time spent in His presence.

5. Revealing Obedience to the Father's Will

Finally, Christ's obedience exemplifies what it means to live under God's authority as our Heavenly Father. In John 6:38, He states unequivocally: "For I have come down from heaven not to do my will but to do the will of him who sent me." Even when faced with suffering in Gethsemane (Matthew 26:39), Jesus submits completely to God's plan for salvation.

This perfect obedience serves as both a revelation of God's purpose for humanity—to live according to His will—and an example for believers striving toward spiritual maturity under their Father's guidance.

Conclusion

In conclusion, Jesus Christ serves as the ultimate revelation of God the Father, bridging the gap between humanity and divinity. Through His life, teachings, and sacrificial death, Jesus not only demonstrated the Father's immense love but also provided a clear path for us to understand and access Him. As stated in John 14:9, "Anyone who has seen me has seen the Father," Jesus embodies the character, will, and heart of God. By studying His actions and words, we gain insight into the Father's nature—His compassion, justice, mercy, and desire for a relationship with His children.

Moreover, through Christ's role as mediator (1 Timothy 2:5), believers are invited into an intimate relationship with God that transcends earthly limitations. This relationship is not based on fear or obligation but on love and grace. Jesus' sacrifice on the cross underscores this truth: that God so loved the world He gave His only Son (John 3:16). In doing so, He opened the door for all who believe to become children of God (John 1:12).

Ultimately, understanding Jesus' role in revealing the Father transforms our spiritual identity. It calls us to live as reflections of God's love and truth in a world often clouded by lies and misconceptions about Him. By embracing Christ's example and teachings, we align ourselves with the eternal truth that God is our one true Father—loving, sovereign, and ever-present in our lives.

Chapter 5: Matthew 23:9 and the Call to Recognize God as Father

In Matthew 23:9, Jesus delivers a profound and often misunderstood command: "And do not call anyone on earth 'father,' for you have one Father, and he is in heaven." This verse challenges readers to examine their spiritual priorities and allegiances, urging them to recognize God as the ultimate authority and source of guidance. To fully understand this teaching, it is essential to explore its context, implications, and how it shapes our relationship with God.

The Context of Matthew 23:9

The statement in Matthew 23:9 is part of a larger discourse where Jesus critiques the religious leaders of His time—specifically the Pharisees and teachers of the law. In this chapter, Jesus warns against their hypocrisy, pride, and desire for titles that elevate them above others. He condemns their actions as self-serving rather than God-serving, highlighting how they seek honor from men instead of directing people toward God.

By instructing His followers not to call anyone on earth "father" in a spiritual sense, Jesus emphasizes that no human being should take the place of God in our lives. This does not mean we should disregard or disrespect our earthly parents; rather, it underscores that our ultimate loyalty belongs to God alone. Earthly relationships are important but must never overshadow our relationship with our Heavenly Father.

Understanding "Father" in a Spiritual Context

The term "father" carries significant weight in both cultural and spiritual contexts. In many societies, fathers are seen as providers, protectors, and sources of wisdom. Spiritually speaking, however, only God embodies these roles perfectly. While earthly fathers may fail or fall short due to human limitations, God's fatherhood is flawless and eternal.

Jesus' teaching in Matthew 23:9 invites believers to shift their focus from earthly figures who may claim spiritual authority to the one true Father who reigns in heaven. This shift requires humility and discernment—qualities that enable us to recognize God's sovereignty over all aspects of life.

The Implications for Believers

Recognizing God as our Father has profound implications for how we live and relate to others:

1. **A Relationship Built on Trust:** Just as children trust their earthly fathers for provision and protection, believers are called to trust God completely. This trust is rooted in His unchanging nature and promises (James 1:17).

2. **Submission to Divine Authority:** Acknowledging God as Father means submitting to His will above all else. This includes obeying His commandments and seeking His guidance through prayer and scripture (Proverbs 3:5-6).

3. **Freedom from Idolatry:** By recognizing God as the ultimate authority, we free ourselves from placing undue reliance on human leaders or institutions. This safeguards us against idolatry—a sin that diverts our worship away from God (Exodus 20:3).

4. **Unity Among Believers:** When we see ourselves as children of the same Heavenly Father, it fosters unity within the body of Christ. This perspective helps us overcome divisions based on race, nationality, or social status (Galatians 3:28).

Practical Applications

To live out the truth of Matthew 23:9 requires intentionality in several areas:

- **Evaluate Your Loyalties:** Reflect on whether there are individuals or institutions you rely on more than God for spiritual guidance or validation.

- **Prioritize Prayer:** Cultivate a habit of turning to your Heavenly Father first when faced with decisions or challenges.

- **Study Scripture:** Deepen your understanding of God›s character by immersing yourself in His Word.

- **Honor Earthly Relationships Appropriately:** While

recognizing God›s ultimate authority, continue to respect and honor your earthly parents as commanded in Exodus 20:12.

Conclusion

Matthew 23:9 serves as a powerful reminder that our primary allegiance must always be to God as our Heavenly Father. By embracing this truth, we align ourselves with His divine purpose and experience the fullness of life He offers through Jesus Christ. As Apostle Bill Amor eloquently explains in *Who Is My Father?*, living under God's fatherly care transforms us into children of truth—individuals who reflect His love and righteousness in a world desperate for hope.

Chapter 6: Earthly Fathers vs. The Heavenly Father: A Biblical Perspective

The concept of fatherhood is deeply ingrained in human experience, serving as a cornerstone for family structure and societal stability. However, when we examine the role of earthly fathers in light of the Bible's teachings about God as our Heavenly Father, we uncover profound differences that highlight God's perfection and ultimate authority. This chapter explores these distinctions, emphasizing how understanding God as the ultimate Father transforms our spiritual lives.

The Role of Earthly Fathers

Earthly fathers play an essential role in nurturing, guiding, and providing for their children. Scripture acknowledges this responsibility and offers guidance on how fathers should lead their families. For instance, Ephesians 6:4 instructs fathers to "bring them up in the training and instruction of the Lord." Similarly, Proverbs 22:6 advises parents to "train up a child in the way he should go; even when he is old he will not depart from it."

Despite these biblical ideals, earthly fathers are inherently flawed due to human sinfulness (Romans 3:23). They may fail to provide adequate love or guidance, make mistakes in judgment, or struggle with personal shortcomings that affect their ability to parent effectively. These imperfections can lead to strained relationships or even feelings of abandonment among children.

The Perfection of the Heavenly Father

In contrast to earthly fathers, God as our Heavenly Father embodies perfect love, wisdom, and provision. Jesus highlights this distinction in Matthew 7:11 when He says, "If you then, who are evil, know how to give good gifts to your children, how much more will your Father who is in heaven give good things to those who ask Him!" This verse underscores God's infinite capacity to care for His children far beyond what any human parent could achieve.

God's fatherhood is marked by several key attributes:

1. **Unconditional Love**: Unlike human love that can be conditional or inconsistent, God's love is steadfast and unchanging. John 3:16 declares His immense love for humanity by giving His only Son so that believers might have eternal life.

2. **Perfect Discipline:** Hebrews 12:6 reminds us that "the Lord disciplines the one He loves." God's correction is always aimed at our growth and well-being rather than stemming from frustration or anger.

3. **Eternal Provision:** While earthly fathers may provide material needs temporarily, God supplies both physical necessities (Matthew 6:31-33) and spiritual sustenance (Philippians 4:19) eternally.

4. **Impartial Justice:** Earthly fathers may show favoritism or act unjustly at times; however, Deuteronomy

32:4 describes God as "a faithful God who does no wrong."

Recognizing God's Sovereignty Over Earthly Relationships

One of the most striking teachings about fatherhood comes from Jesus' words in Matthew 23:9: "And call no man your father on earth, for you have one Father, who is in heaven." This statement does not negate the importance of biological or adoptive fathers but rather emphasizes God's ultimate authority over all familial relationships.

By recognizing God as our true Father:

- We align ourselves with His divine purpose rather than being overly reliant on flawed human figures.

- We find healing from past wounds caused by imperfect parenting through His perfect love.

- We gain clarity on our identity as His children (Galatians 3:26), which transcends any earthly relationship.

Luke 14:26 Earthly Fathers vs. The Heavenly Father: A Biblical Perspective

Luke 14:26 states, *"If anyone comes to me and does not hate father and mother, wife and children, brothers and sisters—yes, even their own life—such a person cannot be my disciple."* This verse is often misunderstood due to its strong language, but when interpreted in the context of biblical teachings, it provides profound insight into the relationship between earthly familial ties and our ultimate allegiance to God as our Heavenly Father.

In Chapter 6 of "Who is My Father?" by Apostle Bill Amor, the discussion focuses on contrasting earthly fathers with the perfection of the Heavenly Father. Luke 14:26 serves as a pivotal scripture for understanding this dynamic. Jesus uses hyperbolic language here—not to advocate literal hatred toward family members—but to emphasize the necessity of prioritizing one's relationship with God above all other relationships. This teaching aligns perfectly with the chapter's theme, which explores how earthly fathers, despite their best intentions, are fallible and limited compared to God's perfect love, guidance, and authority.

Key Points Relating Luke 14:26 to Chapter 6:

1. **Prioritizing God Above All Else**
   The verse underscores that discipleship requires an unwavering commitment to God that surpasses all other loyalties. While earthly fathers may provide care and guidance, they cannot fulfill the role of the ultimate spiritual authority in a believer's life. Chapter 6 highlights this distinction by pointing out that earthly fathers are human and prone to error, whereas God's fatherhood is flawless and eternal.

2. **The Call to Radical Allegiance**
   Jesus' statement in Luke 14:26 challenges believers

to examine where their true allegiance lies. In many cultures, loyalty to family can sometimes conflict with obedience to God's will. For example, if an earthly father discourages a child from following Christ or adhering to biblical principles, this verse reminds believers that their primary duty is to obey God rather than man (Acts 5:29). Chapter 6 delves into such scenarios by illustrating how God's authority must take precedence over any conflicting demands from earthly relationships.

3. **Earthly Fathers as Temporary Stewards**
   Another key aspect discussed in Chapter 6 is the temporary nature of earthly fatherhood compared to the eternal fatherhood of God. Earthly fathers are entrusted with raising their children in accordance with biblical principles (Ephesians 6:4), but they are ultimately stewards under God's supreme authority. Luke 14:26 reinforces this idea by reminding believers that their ultimate identity and purpose are rooted in their relationship with God—not in familial ties.

4. **Sacrificial Love vs. Misplaced Loyalty**
   While honoring one's parents is a biblical command (Exodus 20:12), Luke 14:26 clarifies that honoring does not mean placing them above God or compromising one's faith for their sake. Chapter 6 explores how misplaced loyalty can lead individuals away from truth and righteousness if they prioritize pleasing earthly fathers over obeying their Heavenly Father.

5. **God as the Perfect Model of Fatherhood**
   Finally, Luke 14:26 invites readers to reflect on what it means for God to be our ultimate Father. Unlike earthly fathers who may fail us or lead us astray due

to human limitations, God's love is unconditional, His wisdom is infinite, and His guidance is always perfect (James 1:17). Chapter 6 emphasizes that recognizing this truth allows believers to navigate complex family dynamics while remaining steadfast in their faith.

Conclusion Luke 14:26 Earthly Fathers vs. The Heavenly Father: A Biblical Perspective

Luke 14:26 serves as a powerful reminder that discipleship requires total devotion to Christ—even when it means re-evaluating deeply ingrained cultural or familial expectations. In relation to Chapter 6 of "Who is My Father?", this verse highlights the importance of distinguishing between temporary earthly relationships and the eternal relationship we have with our Heavenly Father. By prioritizing God above all else, believers can experience true freedom and fulfillment as children of the one true King.

Living as Children of the Heavenly Father

Understanding the distinction between earthly fathers and our Heavenly Father calls us to live differently:

1. **Embrace Humility:** Acknowledge that no human relationship can fully satisfy our need for guidance and security—only God can fulfill this role.

2. **Seek Reconciliation:** If past hurts from an earthly fa-

ther linger, bring them before God in prayer and seek His healing power (Psalm 147:3).

3. **Reflect His Love:** As children of God, we are called to emulate His character by extending grace and forgiveness toward others—including our earthly parents (Colossians 3:13).

In conclusion, while earthly fathers serve an important role within God's design for families, they cannot compare to the perfection of our Heavenly Father. By shifting our focus toward Him as the ultimate source of love and authority, we experience a deeper sense of belonging and purpose that shapes every aspect of our lives.

Chapter 7: Spiritual Authority and God's Sovereignty Over All Relationships

In this chapter, we delve into the profound teaching of Jesus Christ as recorded in Matthew 23:9, where He instructs His followers, "And do not call anyone on earth 'father,' for you have one Father, and he is in heaven." This verse challenges us to reflect deeply on the nature of spiritual authority and God's ultimate sovereignty over all relationships. It is a call to recognize that while earthly relationships are important and ordained by God, they must never supersede or replace our relationship with Him as our Heavenly Father.

Understanding Matthew 23:9 in Context

To fully grasp the meaning of Matthew 23:9, it is essential to consider its context. In this passage, Jesus addresses the Pharisees and teachers of the law, who were known for their hypocrisy and desire for titles that elevated their status among people. They sought honorific titles such as "Rabbi" or "Father" to assert their authority over others. Jesus rebukes this practice, emphasizing that true authority belongs solely to God.

By instructing His disciples not to call anyone on earth "father" in a spiritual sense, Jesus was not dismissing the role of biological fathers or mentors but rather pointing to the ultimate source of spiritual guidance—God Himself. This teaching underscores the principle that no human being should take a position in our lives that rivals or replaces God's authority.

The Sovereignty of God Over Earthly Relationships

The Bible consistently teaches that God is sovereign over all creation, including human relationships. As our Creator and Sustainer, He holds ultimate authority over every aspect of our lives. This truth is beautifully illustrated in passages such as Isaiah 45:5-6, where God declares, "I am the Lord, and there is no other; apart from me there is no God."

When we acknowledge God's sovereignty over our relationships, we begin to see them through a divine lens. Earthly relationships—whether with parents, spouses, children, or mentors—are gifts from God meant to reflect His love and character. However, these relationships must always be subordinate to our relationship with Him.

Balancing Earthly Roles with Divine Authority

One might wonder how to reconcile the biblical commandment to honor one's father and mother (Exodus 20:12) with Jesus' instruction in Matthew 23:9. The answer lies in understanding the hierarchy of authority established by God. While we are called to respect and honor those in positions of authority—such as parents or leaders—we must never elevate them above God or allow them to dictate our spiritual beliefs contrary to His Word.

For example, when Peter and the apostles were commanded by religious authorities to stop preaching about Jesus Christ, they boldly replied, "We must obey God rather than human beings!" (Acts 5:29). This response demonstrates that while we are called to respect earthly authorities, our ultimate allegiance belongs to God alone.

Recognizing False Authorities

In a world filled with competing voices claiming authority over our lives—whether cultural norms, political ideologies, or even religious leaders—it is crucial for believers to discern true spiritual authority. The Bible warns against false teachers who distort God's Word for personal gain (2 Peter 2:1-3). These individuals often seek power and recognition rather than pointing others toward Christ.

To guard against false authorities, believers must ground themselves in Scripture as the ultimate standard of truth (2 Timothy 3:16-17). By doing so, we can discern whether a person's teachings align with God's Word or deviate from it.

Living Under God's Sovereignty

Living under God's sovereignty means submitting every aspect of our lives—including our relationships—to His will. It requires humility and a willingness to prioritize His commands above personal desires or societal expectations. When we do so:

1. **Our Relationships Are Transformed:** Recognizing God's sovereignty allows us to approach relation-

ships with love, grace, and forgiveness modeled after His character.

2. **We Find Freedom from Idolatry:** Placing God at the center of our lives frees us from idolizing people or seeking validation from others.

3. **We Experience True Peace:** Trusting in God's authority brings peace amid relational conflicts because we know He is ultimately in control.

Conclusion

Matthew 23:9 serves as a powerful reminder that God alone deserves our highest honor and allegiance. While earthly relationships play an important role in shaping us spiritually and emotionally, they must never overshadow our relationship with Him as our Heavenly Father.

As children of truth living under God's sovereign care, let us strive daily to align ourselves with His will—not only in how we relate to Him but also in how we interact with others around us. By doing so faithfully through prayerful dependence on Him alone above all else ensures eternal alignment reflecting divine purpose fulfilling kingdom destiny eternally secured forevermore!

Chapter 8: Proverbs 15:5: Wisdom in Embracing Correction

In this chapter, we delve into the profound wisdom encapsulated in Proverbs 15:5, which states: "A fool despises his father's instruction, but whoever heeds reproof is prudent." This verse serves as a cornerstone for understanding the relationship between humanity and God as our ultimate Father. It highlights the importance of humility, teachability, and the willingness to accept correction—qualities that define those who live as children of truth under God's fatherly care.

The Context of Proverbs 15:5

The book of Proverbs is often referred to as a treasure trove of divine wisdom. Authored primarily by King Solomon, it provides practical guidance for living a life that honors God. Proverbs 15:5 specifically contrasts two types of individuals: the fool who rejects instruction and the wise person who embraces reproof. In biblical terms, "instruction" often refers to moral or spiritual guidance, while "reproof" signifies corrective feedback aimed at realigning someone with the path of righteousness.

This verse is particularly relevant when considering our relationship with God as our Heavenly Father. Just as earthly parents correct their children out of love and a desire for their well-being, God disciplines His children to guide them toward spiritual maturity and eternal life.

The Fool Who Rejects Instruction

The first part of Proverbs 15:5 warns against despising a father's instruction. In biblical literature, the term "fool" does not merely describe someone lacking intelligence; rather, it denotes a person who is morally deficient or spiritually blind. A fool resists correction because they are prideful and unwilling to acknowledge their need for guidance.

Rejecting God's instruction can manifest in various ways:

1. **Ignoring Scripture:** The Bible is God›s primary means of instructing His children. When individuals neglect to read or apply its teachings, they effectively reject His guidance.

2. **Resisting Conviction:** The Holy Spirit convicts believers of sin and prompts them to repent. Ignoring this conviction hardens the heart and leads to spiritual stagnation.

3. **Disregarding Wise Counsel:** God often uses other believers—pastors, mentors, or friends—to provide correction. Dismissing their advice can result in missed opportunities for growth.

The consequences of rejecting God's instruction are severe. Proverbs 14:12 warns, "There is a way that seems right to a man, but its end is the way to death." By refusing correction, fools set themselves on a path that leads away from God and toward destruction.

The Prudence of Heeding Reproof

In contrast to the fool, Proverbs 15:5 commends those who heed reproof as prudent. Prudence involves exercising sound judgment and foresight—qualities that enable individuals to make wise decisions aligned with God's will.

Heeding reproof requires humility—a recognition that we are fallible beings in need of divine guidance. It also demands trust in God's character as a loving Father who disciplines us for our good (Hebrews 12:6). When we embrace correction with an open heart, several benefits follow:

1. **Spiritual Growth:** Accepting reproof allows us to identify areas where we fall short and make necessary changes to align with God›s standards.

2. **Deeper Relationship with God:** Obedience fosters intimacy with our Heavenly Father by demonstrating our love and reverence for Him (John 14:15).

3. **Protection from Harm:** God›s corrections often serve as warnings that prevent us from making choices with harmful consequences.

4. **Wisdom Acquisition:** As stated in Proverbs 9:9, «Give instruction to a wise man, and he will be still wiser; teach a righteous man, and he will increase in learning.»

Biblical Examples of Embracing Correction

The Bible provides numerous examples of individuals who either embraced or rejected correction—and the outcomes they experienced:

- **David's Repentance (2 Samuel 12):** When confronted by Nathan about his sin with Bathsheba, David humbly acknowledged his wrongdoing and sought forgiveness from God. His response exemplifies how embracing reproof leads to restoration.

- **Jonah's Reluctance (Jonah 1-4):** Initially resistant to God›s command to preach in Nineveh, Jonah eventually obeyed after experiencing divine discipline through being swallowed by a great fish. His story illustrates how God's corrections are designed to redirect us toward fulfilling His purposes.

- **Pharaoh's Hardened Heart (Exodus 7-11):** Despite multiple warnings through Moses and Aaron, Pharaoh repeatedly refused to heed God›s instructions. His stubbornness resulted in devastating plagues upon Egypt—a stark reminder of the dangers associated with rejecting divine correction.

Practical Applications for Modern Believers

As followers of Christ seeking to live as children of truth under God's fatherly care, how can we cultivate an attitude that embraces correction? Here are some practical steps:

1. **Study Scripture Regularly:** Immersing ourselves

in God›s Word equips us with knowledge about His expectations and helps us recognize areas where we need improvement.

2. **Pray for Humility:** Ask God for a teachable spirit that willingly accepts His discipline without resentment or resistance.

3. **Seek Accountability:** Surround yourself with mature believers who can provide honest feedback about your spiritual journey.

4. **Reflect on Past Corrections:** Consider times when you have experienced God›s discipline—what lessons did you learn? How did those experiences shape your faith?

5. **Respond Promptly:** When convicted by Scripture or counsel from others regarding sinful behavior or poor decisions—act immediately! Delayed obedience often leads only further astray!

Conclusion

Proverbs 15:5 offers timeless wisdom about embracing correction—a hallmark characteristic distinguishing wise children-of-truth versus foolish followers-of-lies! By humbly accepting both instruction-reproof-from-Heavenly-Father-through-Scripture-Spirit-community-we-grow-spiritually-deepen-intimacy-with-God-protect-against-harm-acquire-wisdom-needed-navigate-life-successfully! Let-us-strive-live-prudently-heeding-reproof-glorifying-Him-every-aspect-lives!

Chapter 9: Fools and the Rejection of Instruction: Lessons from Proverbs

The book of Proverbs, often referred to as the "book of wisdom," is a treasure trove of divine insights into human behavior, morality, and spiritual growth. Among its many themes, one recurring motif is the contrast between wisdom and folly. Proverbs 15:5 states, "A fool despises his father's instruction, but whoever heeds reproof is prudent." This verse encapsulates a profound truth about the human condition: our response to correction and instruction reveals the state of our hearts and our relationship with God as our ultimate Father.

Understanding the Fool in Biblical Context

In biblical literature, the term "fool" does not merely refer to someone lacking intelligence or education. Instead, it describes a person who rejects wisdom, disregards moral guidance, and lives in defiance of God's will. The fool is characterized by arrogance, stubbornness, and an unwillingness to learn or change. Proverbs 12:15 further elaborates on this idea: "The way of a fool is right in his own eyes, but a wise man listens to advice." This self-assured attitude blinds fools to their need for correction and leads them down paths of destruction.

The rejection of instruction is not merely an intellectual failing; it is a spiritual issue rooted in pride. By refusing to heed correction—whether it comes from earthly parents, mentors, or directly from God's Word—the fool demonstrates a heart that is resistant to God's authority. This resistance ultimately separates them from the blessings and protection that come with living under God's fatherly care.

The Role of Instruction in Spiritual Growth

Instruction and correction are essential components of spiritual growth. Just as earthly parents discipline their children out of love (Hebrews 12:6), so too does God correct His children for their ultimate good. Proverbs 3:11-12 reminds us: "My son, do not despise the Lord's discipline or be weary of His reproof, for the Lord reproves him whom He loves, as a father the son in whom he delights."

For those who accept God's instruction with humility and openness, correction becomes a pathway to wisdom and maturity. It refines character, aligns priorities with God's will, and fosters deeper intimacy with Him. In contrast, those who reject instruction cut themselves off from these benefits and risk falling into greater folly.

Practical Applications for Believers

1. **Cultivating Humility:** To avoid the pitfalls of foolishness, believers must cultivate humility—a willingness to admit mistakes and learn from them. James 4:6 reminds us that «God opposes the proud but gives grace to the humble.» By acknowledging our need for guidance and correction, we position ourselves to receive God›s grace and grow in

wisdom.

2. **Seeking Wise Counsel:** Surrounding oneself with godly mentors and advisors can provide valuable perspective and accountability. Proverbs 11:14 states, «Where there is no guidance, a people fall; but in an abundance of counselors there is safety." Seeking advice from those who are grounded in Scripture helps guard against blind spots and poor decisions.

3. **Embracing Discipline as Love:** Rather than viewing correction as punitive or harsh, believers should see it as an expression of God›s love and care. Hebrews 12:11 acknowledges that discipline may be painful at the moment but ultimately yields "the peaceful fruit of righteousness" for those trained by it.

4. **Meditating on Scripture:** Regular engagement with God›s Word equips believers with wisdom for daily living (Psalm 119:105). By internalizing biblical principles, we develop discernment that enables us to recognize folly when it arises—both within ourselves and others.

Jesus Christ: The Ultimate Model of Wisdom

Jesus Christ embodies perfect wisdom (Colossians 2:3) and serves as our ultimate example of submission to God's instruction. Throughout His earthly ministry, Jesus consistently sought His Father's will above all else (John 5:19). Even when faced with suffering on the cross—a form of divine discipline borne out of love for humanity—He remained obedient unto death (Philippians 2:8).

As followers of Christ, we are called to emulate His example by submitting ourselves fully to God's authority. This includes embracing correction as part of our sanctification process—a journey toward becoming more like Christ each day.

Conclusion

Proverbs 15:5 offers timeless wisdom about the importance of accepting instruction rather than rejecting it like fools do. By humbling ourselves before God's Word—and being open to reproof from trusted sources—we align ourselves with His purposes for our lives while avoiding many pitfalls associated with folly.

Ultimately though difficult at times embracing corrections refines us into better reflections Of Christ Himself .

Chapter 10: Humility as a Mark of the Children of Truth

Humility is one of the most profound and essential characteristics that define those who live as children of truth under God's fatherly care. It is a quality that not only reflects an individual's acknowledgment of their dependence on God but also serves as a foundation for spiritual growth, obedience, and alignment with divine truth. In this chapter, we will explore the biblical significance of humility, its role in shaping our identity as children of God, and how it contrasts with pride—a trait often associated with those who reject correction and divine authority.

The Biblical Foundation of Humility

The Bible consistently emphasizes humility as a virtue that pleases God and draws us closer to Him. James 4:6 states, "God opposes the proud but gives grace to the humble." This verse highlights the stark contrast between pride and humility, showing that while pride creates a barrier between humanity and God, humility opens the door to His grace and favor. Similarly, Proverbs 22:4 teaches that "Humility is the fear of the Lord; its wages are riches and honor and life." This scripture underscores that true humility stems from reverence for God—a recognition of His sovereignty and our position as His creation.

Jesus Christ Himself exemplified perfect humility during His earthly ministry. Philippians 2:5-8 describes how Jesus, though being in very nature God, "made himself nothing by taking the very nature of a servant" and humbled Himself even to the point of death on a cross. As followers of Christ, we are called to emulate this attitude of selflessness and submission to God's will.

Humility as Dependence on God

One key aspect of humility is acknowledging our complete dependence on God for everything—our existence, salvation, wisdom, strength, and guidance. John 15:5 records Jesus saying, "Apart from me you can do nothing." This statement serves as a reminder that all human efforts are ultimately futile without God's enabling power. Children of truth recognize this reality and live in constant reliance on their Heavenly Father.

This dependence manifests in various ways: through prayer (acknowledging our need for God's intervention), obedience (submitting to His commands), and gratitude (recognizing His provision). By contrast, those who reject God's authority often exhibit self-reliance or arrogance—traits that lead them away from truth.

The Role of Humility in Receiving Correction

Proverbs 15:5 states, "A fool spurns his father's discipline, but whoever heeds correction shows prudence." This verse highlights another critical dimension of humility: the willingness to accept correction. As children under God's care, we must be open to His reproof—whether it comes through Scripture, circumstances, or other believers. Such openness requires humility because it involves admitting our mistakes and submitting to God's wisdom over our own understanding.

In Hebrews 12:6-7, we are reminded that "the Lord disciplines the one he loves," treating us as His children when He corrects us. Far from being punitive or harsh, divine discipline is an expression of God's love aimed at refining us into His likeness. Humble individuals embrace this process because they trust in their Father's good intentions.

Contrasting Humility with Pride

Pride stands in direct opposition to humility—it is characterized by self-exaltation rather than submission to God. Proverbs 16:18 warns that "Pride goes before destruction," illustrating how this trait leads individuals away from truth toward spiritual ruin. Pride blinds people to their need for God's guidance; it fosters rebellion against His authority while promoting self-centeredness.

In contrast to proud individuals who reject correction (Proverbs 15:10), humble believers welcome instruction because they value growth over ego preservation. They understand that true wisdom comes not from asserting independence but from aligning themselves with divine truth.

Cultivating Humility as Children of Truth

Becoming humble requires intentional effort—it does not come naturally due to humanity's fallen nature (Romans 3:23). However, through prayerful dependence on God's Spirit working within us (Galatians 5:22-23), we can cultivate this virtue over time:

1. **Meditate on Scripture** – Regularly reading passages about humility helps shape our mindset according to biblical principles.

2. **Pray for Transformation** – Ask God daily for help in overcoming prideful tendencies while developing Christlike qualities.

3. **Serve Others Selflessly** – Following Jesus› example by putting others› needs above our own fosters genuine humility.

4. **Accept Feedback Graciously** – Viewing criticism constructively rather than defensively demonstrates maturity rooted in trust toward God›s plan.

By practicing these habits consistently undergirded by faith-filled dependence upon Him alone—not ourselves—we grow increasingly reflective mirrors bearing witness unto His glory!

Conclusion for Chapter 10: Humility as a Mark of the Children of Truth

In conclusion, humility is not merely an admirable trait but a defining characteristic of those who live as children of truth under God's fatherly care. It is through humility that we acknowledge our dependence on God, recognize His sovereignty, and submit to His divine will. The Bible consistently teaches that God opposes the proud but gives grace to the humble (James 4:6). This grace enables believers to grow in wisdom, embrace correction, and walk in alignment with His truth.

Humility also fosters a teachable spirit, allowing us to accept reproof and guidance from both Scripture and godly counsel. Proverbs 15:5 reminds us that rejecting correction is the mark of a fool, while embracing it demonstrates wisdom. As children of truth, our willingness to be corrected reflects our trust in God's perfect plan for our lives and our desire to become more like Christ.

Ultimately, humility draws us closer to the Father by breaking down barriers of pride and self-reliance. It opens our hearts to experience His love more fully and equips us to extend that love to others. By cultivating humility, we not only honor God as our ultimate Father but also reflect His character in a world desperately in need of His truth and grace. Let us strive daily to walk humbly with our God (Micah 6:8), knowing that He exalts those who humble themselves before Him (Matthew 23:12).

Chapter 11: Living Under God's Fatherly Care: A Life of Obedience

Living under God's fatherly care is a profound privilege that comes with both blessings and responsibilities. As the ultimate Father, God provides not only love and guidance but also correction and discipline to shape His children into individuals who reflect His character. This chapter explores what it means to live a life of obedience under God's care, drawing from biblical principles and examples to illustrate how this relationship transforms every aspect of our lives.

Understanding God's Fatherly Role

The Bible consistently portrays God as a loving yet authoritative Father who desires the best for His children. In Hebrews 12:5-6, we read, *"My son, do not regard lightly the discipline of the Lord, nor be weary when reproved by him. For the Lord disciplines the one he loves, and chastises every son whom he receives."* This passage highlights an essential aspect of God's fatherhood: His discipline is an expression of His love. Just as earthly parents correct their children to guide them toward maturity, God disciplines us to help us grow in holiness (Hebrews 12:10).

God's care extends beyond discipline; He also provides for our needs, protects us from harm, and leads us on paths of righteousness. Psalm 23 beautifully captures this imagery, describing the Lord as a shepherd who ensures that His sheep lack nothing. Living under God's fatherly care means trusting in His provision and guidance, even when we do not fully understand His plans.

The Call to Obedience

Obedience is a central theme in Scripture and a key component of living under God's care. Jesus Himself emphasized the importance of obedience in John 14:15: *"If you love me, you will keep my commandments."* This statement underscores that obedience is not merely about following rules; it is an expression of our love for God and our acknowledgment of His authority as our Father.

Throughout the Bible, we see examples of individuals who demonstrated obedience to God despite challenges or uncertainties. Abraham's willingness to sacrifice Isaac (Genesis 22) exemplifies unwavering trust in God's plan. Similarly, Noah obeyed God's command to build an ark despite ridicule from others (Genesis 6-7). These stories remind us that obedience often requires faith and courage but ultimately leads to blessings.

The Role of Scripture in Guiding Obedience

To live obediently under God's care, we must know His will—and Scripture is the primary way He reveals it to us. Psalm 119:105 declares, *"Your word is a lamp to my feet and a light to my path."* By studying the Bible regularly, we gain insight into God's commands and principles for living a righteous life.

Scripture also equips us to discern between truth and falsehood. In today's world, where moral relativism often blurs the lines between right and wrong, grounding ourselves in biblical truth helps us remain steadfast in our obedience to God.

The Blessings of Obedience

Obedience brings numerous blessings into our lives. Deuteronomy 28 outlines both the blessings for those who obey God's commands and the consequences for disobedience. Among these blessings are prosperity, protection from enemies, and favor in all areas of life.

However, it is important to note that obedience does not guarantee a life free from difficulties. Jesus warned His disciples that they would face persecution for following Him (John 16:33). Yet even amidst trials, those who live obediently experience peace and joy because they are aligned with God's will.

Overcoming Challenges to Obedience

Living obediently under God's care can be challenging at times due to our human nature and external influences. Temptations abound in various forms—whether through societal pressures or personal desires—that seek to draw us away from God's path.

To overcome these challenges:

1. **Rely on Prayer:** Regular communication with God strengthens our relationship with Him and provides clarity during moments of doubt or temptation.

2. **Seek Accountability:** Surrounding ourselves with fellow believers who encourage us in our walk with Christ helps us stay committed.

3. **Remember God's Promises:** Reflecting on Scriptures like Romans 8:28 *("And we know that in all things God works for the good of those who love him")* reminds us why obedience matters.

Conclusion

Living under God's fatherly care involves embracing both His love and authority through a life marked by obedience. While this journey may involve challenges along the way— such as resisting temptations or enduring hardships—it ultimately leads to spiritual growth and deeper intimacy with our Heavenly Father.

As children of truth called into fellowship with Him through Jesus Christ (John 1:12), let us strive daily toward faithful obedience out of gratitude for all He has done for us! By doing so—not only do we honor Him—but also position ourselves within His perfect plan filled with hope & eternal purpose!

Chapter 12: Children of the Lie: Rejecting Divine Authority

In this chapter, we delve into the profound consequences of rejecting divine authority and how it shapes individuals into what Apostle Bill Amor refers to as "Children of the Lie." This term is not merely a label but a spiritual condition that reflects a life lived in opposition to God's truth. By examining biblical principles and scriptural examples, we will uncover the dangers of rejecting God's authority and the transformative power of embracing His sovereignty.

The Origin of Lies: A Biblical Perspective

The concept of lies and deception finds its roots in the earliest chapters of Scripture. In Genesis 3, we encounter the serpent's cunning deception of Eve in the Garden of Eden. The serpent's question, "Did God really say...?" (Genesis 3:1), represents the first recorded instance of humanity being tempted to doubt God's authority. This act of questioning divine instruction led to humanity's fall into sin—a direct result of choosing to believe a lie over God's truth.

Jesus Himself identifies Satan as "the father of lies" in John 8:44, stating, "He was a murderer from the beginning, not holding to the truth, for there is no truth in him. When he lies, he speaks his native language, for he is a liar and the father of lies." This stark contrast between truth and falsehood underscores the spiritual battle at play when individuals reject divine authority. To reject God's authority is to align oneself with deception and ultimately with Satan's agenda.

Characteristics of Children of the Lie

Apostle Bill Amor emphasizes that those who reject divine authority exhibit certain characteristics that distinguish them as "Children of the Lie." These traits are often rooted in pride, rebellion, and an unwillingness to submit to God's will. Proverbs 15:5 provides insight into this mindset: "A fool spurns a parent's discipline, but whoever heeds correction shows prudence." Just as earthly children who reject parental guidance are considered foolish, so too are those who dismiss God's instruction.

1. **Pride and Self-Reliance**
   One hallmark trait is an inflated sense of self-reliance. Rather than acknowledging their dependence on God, these individuals place their trust in human wisdom or personal achievements. Proverbs 16:18 warns us that "Pride goes before destruction, a haughty spirit before a fall." Pride blinds individuals to their need for divine guidance and leads them further away from truth.

2. **Rebellion Against Authority**
   Rebellion is another defining characteristic. Romans 13:1-2 reminds us that all authority comes from God: "Let everyone be subject to the governing authorities, for there is no authority except that which God has established." To rebel against legitimate authority— whether spiritual or earthly—is ultimately an act of defiance against God Himself.

3. Rejection of Correction

As highlighted in Proverbs 15:5, rejecting correction is indicative of foolishness. Those who refuse to accept reproof or discipline demonstrate an unwillingness to grow spiritually or align themselves with God's will.

4. Embracing Falsehoods

Finally, Children of the Lie are characterized by their acceptance and propagation of falsehoods. Isaiah 5:20 warns against this tendency: "Woe to those who call evil good and good evil." By distorting truth and embracing moral relativism, they further distance themselves from God's unchanging standards.

Consequences of Rejecting Divine Authority

The Bible outlines several consequences for those who choose to live as Children of the Lie:

1. Spiritual Blindness

Rejecting divine authority results in spiritual blindness—a condition where individuals are unable or unwilling to discern truth from falsehood. Second Corinthians 4:4 explains that "The god of this age has blinded the minds of unbelievers so that they cannot see the light of the gospel."

2. Separation from God

Sin creates a barrier between humanity and God (Isaiah 59:2). By rejecting His authority, individuals sever their relationship with Him and risk eternal separation unless they repent.

3. **Eternal Judgment**
   Revelation 21:8 lists liars among those who will face
   eternal judgment in "the fiery lake of burning sulfur."
   This sobering reality underscores the seriousness
   with which God views rejection of His truth.

The Path Back to Truth

Despite these dire consequences, Scripture offers hope for
redemption through repentance and submission to God's
authority:

1. **Acknowledging Sin**
   The first step toward restoration is acknowledging
   one's sinfulness (1 John 1:9). Confession paves the
   way for forgiveness and reconciliation with God.

2. **Submitting to Christ's Lordship**
   True freedom comes from submitting fully to Christ as
   Lord (John 8:32). By aligning oneself with His teachings and accepting His sacrifice on the cross, believers can break free from deception.

3. **Living by God's Word**
   Psalm 119:105 describes God's Word as "a lamp for
   my feet"—a guiding light that leads believers out of
   darkness into truth.

Conclusion

Rejecting divine authority may offer temporary gratification
or autonomy but ultimately leads down a path fraught with
spiritual peril. As Apostle Bill Amor eloquently states in *Who*

Is My Father?, "To live apart from God's truth is not merely misguided; it is catastrophic." By recognizing our dependence on Him and embracing His sovereignty over our lives, we can transition from being Children of the Lie to becoming Children of Truth—heirs to His eternal kingdom.

Chapter 13: Contrasting Truth and Lies in Spiritual Identity Formation

In this chapter, we delve into the critical role that truth and lies play in shaping our spiritual identity. The Bible consistently emphasizes the importance of aligning ourselves with truth, as it is foundational to understanding who we are in relation to God. Conversely, embracing lies leads to spiritual confusion, separation from God, and ultimately a distorted sense of self. By examining key scriptures and biblical principles, we will uncover how truth serves as the cornerstone of our identity as children of God and how lies can derail us from fulfilling our divine purpose.

The Foundation of Truth in Spiritual Identity

The concept of truth is central to the Christian faith. Jesus Himself declared in John 14:6, "I am the way, the truth, and the life. No one comes to the Father except through Me." This statement underscores that truth is not merely a set of abstract principles but is embodied in the person of Jesus Christ. To form a spiritual identity rooted in truth, one must first recognize Jesus as the ultimate source of truth.

John 8:31-32 further reinforces this idea: "If you abide in My word, you are My disciples indeed. And you shall know the truth, and the truth shall make you free." Here, Jesus links freedom—both spiritual and personal—to knowing and living by His Word. A life grounded in God's truth liberates us from sin's bondage and provides clarity about our purpose as God's children.

Lies: The Enemy's Tool for Distortion

In stark contrast to truth stands deception, which originates from Satan—the father of lies (John 8:44). From the very beginning, Satan has used lies to undermine humanity's relationship with God. In Genesis 3:1-5, we see how he deceived Eve by twisting God's words, leading her to doubt God's goodness and disobey His command. This act of deception not only disrupted humanity's fellowship with God but also introduced sin into the world.

Lies continue to be a powerful tool that distorts spiritual identity today. They manifest in various forms—false teachings, cultural relativism, self-deception—and lead individuals away from God's intended path for their lives. For example:

- **False Teachings:** These distortions often masquerade as biblical truths but contradict Scripture when examined closely (2 Peter 2:1). They can lead believers astray by promoting ideas that prioritize human desires over God›s will.

- **Cultural Relativism:** This philosophy suggests that there is no absolute truth and that morality is subjective. Such thinking directly opposes biblical teachings like Psalm 119:160 («The entirety of Your word is truth»).

- **Self-Deception:** James 1:22 warns against being hearers of the Word without acting on it: «But be doers of the word, and not hearers only, deceiving yourselves.» Failing to live out biblical truths results in a fragmented spiritual identity.

The Role of Scripture in Discerning Truth

To combat lies and build a strong spiritual identity rooted in truth, believers must immerse themselves in Scripture. As Paul writes in 2 Timothy 3:16-17: "All Scripture is given by inspiration of God and is profitable for doctrine, for reproof, for correction, for instruction in righteousness." The Bible serves as an authoritative guide that helps us discern between truth and falsehood.

Psalm 119:105 beautifully illustrates this point: "Your word is a lamp to my feet and a light to my path." Just as a lamp illuminates darkness, God's Word exposes lies and guides us toward righteousness.

Living as Children of Truth

Living as children of truth requires more than intellectual assent; it demands active obedience to God's commands. Ephesians 4:25 urges believers to "put away lying" and instead "speak each one truth with his neighbor." This call extends beyond honesty—it encompasses living authentically according to God's standards.

Furthermore, humility plays a crucial role in embracing correction when confronted with areas where we've believed or acted upon lies (Proverbs 15:5). A wise person acknowledges their need for growth under God's fatherly care.

Conclusion

Contrasting truth with lies reveals how pivotal these forces are in shaping our spiritual identities. While lies seek to distort our understanding of who we are before God—leading us down paths marked by confusion—truth anchors us firmly within His love and purpose for our lives.

As Apostle Bill Amor emphasizes throughout *Who Is My Father?*, recognizing God as our ultimate Father equips us with clarity about our true identity while empowering us against deception's snares. By abiding steadfastly within His Word—the embodiment of eternal Truth—we align ourselves fully with Him who calls us His beloved children.

Chapter 14: The Power of Reproof: Learning from God's Discipline

The concept of reproof and discipline is central to understanding the relationship between God and His children. Throughout Scripture, God is portrayed as a loving Father who disciplines those He loves, not out of anger or malice, but out of a desire to guide His children toward righteousness and spiritual maturity. In this chapter, we will explore the biblical foundation for divine discipline, its purpose in the life of believers, and how embracing correction can lead to profound spiritual growth.

Understanding Divine Discipline

The Bible makes it clear that discipline is an expression of God's love. In Hebrews 12:6-7, we read: *"For the Lord disciplines the one He loves, and chastises every son whom He receives. It is for discipline that you have to endure. God is treating you as sons. For what son is there whom his father does not discipline?"* This passage emphasizes that God›s correction is not punitive but restorative. Just as a loving earthly father corrects his child to teach them right from wrong, so too does our Heavenly Father correct us to align us with His will.

Proverbs 3:11-12 echoes this sentiment: *"My son, do not despise the Lord's discipline or be weary of His reproof, for the Lord reproves him whom He loves, as a father the son in whom he delights."* Here, we see that reproof is not something to be feared or resented but rather embraced as evidence of God's care and delight in us.

The Purpose of Reproof

God's discipline serves several purposes in the lives of believers:

1. **Correction:** One of the primary purposes of divine reproof is to correct our behavior when we stray from God›s path. Psalm 119:67 says, *"Before I was afflicted I went astray, but now I keep Your word."* Through correction, God brings us back into alignment with His truth.

2. **Spiritual Growth:** Discipline helps us grow in holiness and maturity. Hebrews 12:10 states, *"He disciplines us for our good, that we may share His holiness."* By enduring God›s correction, we are refined and transformed into His likeness.

3. **Protection:** Sometimes God›s discipline protects us from greater harm by steering us away from destructive choices or behaviors. Proverbs 15:5 reminds us that *"A fool despises his father's instruction, but whoever heeds reproof is prudent."* Listening to God›s correction can save us from unnecessary pain and consequences.

4. **Strengthening Faith:** Trials and discipline often test our faith, but they also strengthen it. James 1:2-4 encourages believers to *"count it all joy when you meet trials of various kinds,"* knowing that these challenges produce steadfastness and maturity.

Responding to God's Reproof

How we respond to God's discipline reveals much about our spiritual condition. Proverbs 12:1 bluntly states, *"Whoever loves discipline loves knowledge, but he who hates reproof is stupid."* A wise person recognizes the value of correction and humbly submits to it.

Here are some practical ways believers can respond to divine reproof:

1. **Examine Your Heart:** When faced with correction—whether through Scripture, circumstances, or other means—take time to reflect on your actions and attitudes. Ask God to reveal any areas where you need repentance or change (Psalm 139:23-24).

2. **Embrace Humility:** Accepting reproof requires humility and a willingness to admit when you're wrong. James 4:6 reminds us that *"God opposes the proud but gives grace to the humble."*

3. **Seek Wisdom:** Turn to Scripture for guidance on how to align your life with God›s will (2 Timothy 3:16). Surround yourself with godly mentors who can provide counsel and encouragement during times of correction (Proverbs 27:17).

4. **Trust in God's Love:** Remember that God›s discipline is motivated by love and a desire for your ultimate good (Romans 8:28). Trust that He knows what is best for you even when it's difficult to understand.

The Blessings of Discipline

While enduring reproof may be uncomfortable or even painful at times, it ultimately leads to blessings in our lives:

- **Peaceful Fruit of Righteousness:** Hebrews 12:11 assures us that *"For the moment all discipline seems painful rather than pleasant, but later it yields the peaceful fruit of righteousness to those who have been trained by it."*

- **Closer Relationship with God:** As we submit to His correction and grow in holiness, our relationship with God deepens (John 15:1-2).

- **Eternal Rewards:** Revelation 3:19-21 highlights Jesus› call for repentance through loving rebuke and promises eternal rewards for those who overcome.

Conclusion

God's reproof is a powerful tool for shaping us into the people He created us to be—holy, righteous, and fully devoted followers of Christ. While it may be challenging at times to accept correction or endure trials brought about by divine discipline, we can take comfort in knowing that these experiences are evidence of God's love for us as His children.

As Proverbs 15:31 beautifully puts it: *"The ear that listens to life-giving reproof will dwell among the wise."* Let us strive always to listen attentively when our Heavenly Father speaks words of correction into our lives so that we may grow closer each day toward becoming true reflections of His glory.

Chapter 15: Aligning with Righteousness Through Submission to God's Will

The concept of aligning with righteousness through submission to God's will is one of the most profound and transformative themes in the Bible. It challenges believers to surrender their personal desires, ambitions, and even their understanding of what is right, in favor of trusting and obeying the divine plan laid out by God. This chapter explores how submission to God's will not only aligns us with His righteousness but also deepens our relationship with Him as our Heavenly Father.

Understanding Righteousness in Biblical Terms

Righteousness, as defined in scripture, refers to being in right standing with God. It is not merely about adhering to a set of moral rules or performing good deeds; rather, it is about living in harmony with God's character and His commands. The Bible teaches that true righteousness comes from faith and obedience to God. For example, Genesis 15:6 states that Abraham "believed the Lord, and He credited it to him as righteousness." This verse highlights that righteousness begins with faith—a trust in God's promises and His ultimate authority.

In the New Testament, Jesus Christ embodies perfect righteousness. Through His life, death, and resurrection, He provides a model for believers to follow. As stated in 2 Corinthians 5:21: "God made Him who had no sin to be sin for us so that in Him we might become the righteousness of God." This passage underscores that aligning with righteousness involves accepting Christ's sacrifice and allowing His Spirit to guide our lives.

Submission as a Pathway to Righteousness

Submission is often misunderstood as weakness or passivity; however, biblical submission is an active choice to yield one's will to God's authority. It requires humility and trust—qualities that are essential for spiritual growth. James 4:7 instructs believers: "Submit yourselves therefore to God. Resist the devil, and he will flee from you." This verse reveals a powerful truth: submission to God empowers us to resist evil and align ourselves with His righteous purposes.

Jesus Himself exemplified perfect submission during His earthly ministry. In Luke 22:42, as He prayed in the Garden of Gethsemane before His crucifixion, Jesus said: "Father, if You are willing, take this cup from Me; yet not My will but Yours be done." Despite facing immense suffering, Jesus chose obedience over self-preservation—a decision that ultimately fulfilled God's redemptive plan for humanity.

The Role of Obedience in Aligning with God's Will

Obedience is a tangible expression of submission. It demonstrates our willingness to trust God's wisdom above our own understanding. Proverbs 3:5-6 advises: "Trust in the Lord with all your heart and lean not on your own understanding; in all your ways submit to Him, and He will make your paths straight." By obeying God's commands—even when they challenge our preferences or logic—we position ourselves under His guidance and protection.

One notable example of obedience leading to alignment with righteousness can be found in the story of Noah (Genesis 6-9). When instructed by God to build an ark despite no visible signs of impending floodwaters, Noah obeyed without hesitation. His faith-driven actions not only saved his family but also preserved humanity's future—a testament to how submission can lead to blessings beyond comprehension.

Overcoming Barriers to Submission

While submission is essential for aligning with righteousness, it is not always easy. Human pride often resists yielding control; fear may cause hesitation; doubt can undermine trust in God's plan. To overcome these barriers:

1. **Cultivate Humility:** Recognize that God›s wisdom surpasses human understanding (Isaiah 55:8-9).

2. **Strengthen Faith:** Meditate on scriptures that affirm God›s faithfulness (Romans 8:28).

3. **Pray for Guidance:** Seek clarity through prayer when faced with difficult decisions (Philippians 4:6-7).

4. **Surround Yourself With Support:** Engage with fellow believers who encourage accountability

(Hebrews 10:24-25).

The Rewards of Aligning With Righteousness

When we submit ourselves fully to God's will:

- **We Experience Peace:** Trusting God›s sovereignty alleviates anxiety about life›s uncertainties (Philippians 4:7).

- **We Grow Spiritually:** Obedience fosters maturity as we learn dependence on Him (James 1:2-4).

- **We Reflect Christ's Character:** Our lives become testimonies that draw others toward faith (Matthew 5:16).

Ultimately aligning ourselves through submission transforms us into vessels through which God's love flows freely into this world—a reflection not only pleasing unto Him but also impactful upon those around us.

In conclusion aligning oneself righteously entails daily intentionality towards yielding wholly unto divine sovereignty, thereby fostering deeper intimacy between Creator & creation alike ensuring eternal fulfillment therein assuredly promised via scriptural affirmation thereof eternally secured therein.

Chapter 16: The Ultimate Guide: God's Word as a Father's Instruction Manual

The Bible is often referred to as the ultimate guide for life, and for good reason. It is not merely a collection of ancient texts or moral teachings; it is the inspired Word of God, designed to instruct, correct, and guide His children in every aspect of their lives. As Apostle Bill Amor explores in *Who Is My Father?,* understanding God as our ultimate Father also means recognizing His Word as the instruction manual He has lovingly provided for us. This chapter delves into how scripture serves as a comprehensive guide for living a life that honors God and reflects His character.

The Bible: A Father's Love Letter

At its core, the Bible is an expression of God's love for humanity. From Genesis to Revelation, it reveals His plan for creation, redemption, and eternal fellowship with His children. Just as an earthly father provides guidance out of love and concern for his child's well-being, so too does our Heavenly Father offer wisdom through His Word. In John 3:16, we see the depth of this love: "For God so loved the world that He gave His only begotten Son, that whoever believes in Him should not perish but have everlasting life." This verse encapsulates the heart of God's instruction—His desire for us to live in relationship with Him and experience eternal life.

Scripture as a Source of Wisdom and Correction

Proverbs 15:5 states, "A fool despises his father's instruction, but he who receives correction is prudent." This verse highlights two key aspects of God's Word: its role in providing instruction and its function in correcting us when we stray from His path. Just as a loving father disciplines his child to teach them right from wrong, God uses scripture to reprove and refine us. Hebrews 12:6 reminds us that "the Lord disciplines those He loves," emphasizing that correction is not punitive but restorative.

The Bible addresses every area of life—relationships, finances, work ethic, morality, and more—offering timeless principles that lead to flourishing when followed. For example:

- **Relationships:** Ephesians 4:32 teaches us to «be kind to one another, tenderhearted, forgiving one another, even as God in Christ forgave you.»

- **Finances:** Proverbs 22:7 warns that «the borrower is servant to the lender,» encouraging wise financial stewardship.

- **Work Ethic:** Colossians 3:23 instructs us to «work heartily, as for the Lord and not for men.»

By aligning our lives with these principles, we demonstrate our trust in God's wisdom and our willingness to live under His fatherly care.

The Role of Humility in Receiving Instruction

One of the greatest barriers to benefiting from God's Word is pride. Proverbs 15:5 contrasts the attitudes of fools who reject correction with wise individuals who embrace reproof. To fully receive God's guidance, we must approach scripture with humility—a recognition that we do not have all the answers and need divine direction.

Jesus exemplified this humility during His earthly ministry. In John 5:19-20, He stated, "The Son can do nothing by Himself; He can do only what He sees His Father doing." If Jesus Himself relied on the Father's guidance, how much more should we depend on God's Word?

Practical Steps for Using Scripture as an Instruction Manual

To make the most of God's Word as a guide for life:

1. **Study Regularly:** Set aside time each day to read and meditate on scripture. Tools such as study Bibles or commentaries can provide additional insights.

2. **Pray for Understanding:** Ask the Holy Spirit to illuminate passages and reveal their application to your life (John 14:26).

3. **Memorize Key Verses:** Hiding God›s Word in your heart equips you to recall it during times of need (Psalm 119:11).

4. **Apply What You Learn:** James 1:22 reminds us to be doers of the Word—not hearers only.

5. **Seek Accountability:** Share your journey with fellow believers who can encourage you and hold you accountable.

Living Out God's Instructions

Ultimately, following God's Word transforms us into reflections of His character. As Matthew 5:16 encourages us, "Let your light so shine before men that they may see your good works and glorify your Father in heaven." By living according to scripture's teachings, we not only honor our Heavenly Father but also draw others closer to Him.

In conclusion, viewing the Bible as a father's instruction manual changes how we approach it—it becomes less about rules or rituals and more about relationship. Through its pages, we hear our Father's voice calling us into deeper intimacy with Him while equipping us for every good work (2 Timothy 3:16-17). Let us embrace this divine gift with gratitude and commitment so that we may walk confidently as children of truth under our Father's loving guidance.

Chapter 17: Recognizing False Authorities in Light of Matthew 23:9

In Matthew 23:9, Jesus delivers a profound and challenging command to His followers: "And do not call anyone on earth 'father,' for you have one Father, and He is in heaven." This verse is part of a larger discourse where Jesus rebukes the religious leaders of His time—the Pharisees and scribes—for their hypocrisy and misuse of authority. To fully understand this teaching, it is essential to explore its context, implications, and practical applications for believers today.

The Context of Matthew 23:9

Matthew 23 is a chapter filled with sharp criticism from Jesus toward the religious elite. The Pharisees and scribes had positioned themselves as spiritual authorities over the people, demanding respect and obedience while failing to live according to God's standards. They sought titles such as "Rabbi," "Teacher," and "Father" to elevate their status and assert dominance over others. In doing so, they obscured the true source of spiritual authority—God Himself.

When Jesus instructs His followers not to call anyone on earth "father" in a spiritual sense, He is not condemning the use of the term in familial or cultural contexts. Instead, He is addressing the deeper issue of misplaced allegiance. By claiming titles that belong only to God, these leaders were usurping His role as the ultimate Father and guide for His people.

Understanding False Authorities

False authorities are individuals or systems that claim power or influence over others in ways that contradict God's Word. These can manifest in various forms:

1. **Religious Leaders Who Misuse Their Position**
   Throughout history, there have been leaders who exploit their roles for personal gain or control rather than serving as humble shepherds under God's authority. Such individuals often prioritize tradition, legalism, or personal agendas over biblical truth.

2. **Cultural Influences That Contradict Scripture**
   Society often elevates ideologies or figures that promote values contrary to God's teachings. When believers align themselves with these influences without discernment, they risk compromising their faith.

3. **Self-Exaltation**
   Sometimes, false authority arises from within when individuals place their own opinions or desires above God's will. This can lead to prideful independence rather than submission to the Father's guidance.

The Call to Recognize God as the Ultimate Authority

Jesus' teaching in Matthew 23:9 reminds us that all true authority originates from God. As our heavenly Father, He alone has the wisdom, power, and love necessary to guide us perfectly. Recognizing Him as our ultimate authority requires humility and discernment.

1. **Humility Before God**
   Acknowledging God as our Father means surrendering our pride and submitting to His will. This involves trusting His Word as the final standard for truth and righteousness.

2. **Discernment Through Scripture**
   To identify false authorities, believers must be grounded in Scripture. The Bible serves as a lamp to our feet (Psalm 119:105), illuminating the path of truth amidst a world filled with deception.

3. **Evaluating Loyalties**
   Jesus' command challenges us to examine where we place our trust and allegiance. Are we following human traditions or cultural trends at the expense of biblical principles? Are we seeking approval from others instead of living for God's glory?

Practical Applications for Believers Today

1. **Test All Teachings Against Scripture**
   Acts 17:11 commends the Bereans for examining Paul's teachings against Scripture to ensure they aligned with God's truth. Similarly, believers today must evaluate sermons, books, and other sources of spiritual guidance through the lens of God's Word.

2. **Avoid Idolizing Leaders**
   While it is appropriate to respect pastors, mentors, and other spiritual leaders, we must remember that they are fallible humans who serve under God's authority. Placing them on pedestals can lead to disappointment or misplaced faith.

3. **Cultivate a Personal Relationship with God**
   Recognizing God as our Father involves developing an intimate relationship with Him through prayer, worship, and study of His Word. This connection enables us to hear His voice clearly amidst competing influences.

4. **Stand Firm Against Cultural Pressures**
   In an age where relativism and secularism dominate many aspects of society, believers must remain steadfast in their commitment to biblical truth—even when it goes against popular opinion.

5. **Encourage Accountability Within the Church**
   Healthy churches foster environments where leaders are held accountable by fellow believers according to biblical standards (1 Timothy 3:1-13). This helps prevent abuses of power while promoting Christlike leadership.

Conclusion

Matthew 23:9 serves as both a warning against false authorities and an invitation to embrace God as our one true Father in heaven. By recognizing Him as the ultimate source of guidance and rejecting any earthly claims that seek to rival His sovereignty, we align ourselves with truth and righteousness.

As children of the heavenly Father, we are called to live lives marked by humility, discernment, and unwavering loyalty to Him alone. In doing so, we reflect His glory in a world desperately in need of His light—a world where many still search for meaning in places that cannot satisfy.

May this chapter inspire you not only to recognize false authorities but also to deepen your relationship with your heavenly Father—the One who loves you unconditionally and leads you faithfully every step of your journey.

Chapter 18: Trusting in God's Plan as Our True Father in Heaven

The concept of trusting in God's plan is a cornerstone of Christian faith and theology. As believers, we are called to recognize God as our ultimate Father in heaven, whose wisdom and sovereignty surpass all human understanding. This chapter delves into the profound truth that God's plans for His children are always good, even when they may not align with our immediate desires or expectations. By examining key biblical passages and principles, we will explore how trust in God's plan shapes our spiritual identity and strengthens our relationship with Him.

The Sovereignty of God as Our Father

One of the most comforting aspects of viewing God as our Father is His absolute sovereignty over all creation. Unlike earthly fathers who are limited by human frailty, God possesses infinite knowledge, power, and love. Jeremiah 29:11 is a foundational scripture that highlights this truth: *"For I know the plans I have for you," declares the Lord, "plans to prosper you and not to harm you, plans to give you hope and a future."* This verse reassures us that God's intentions toward His children are always rooted in love and goodness.

As our heavenly Father, God orchestrates every detail of our lives according to His divine purpose. Romans 8:28 further emphasizes this point: *"And we know that in all things God works for the good of those who love him, who have been called according to his purpose."* Trusting in this promise requires us to surrender our own understanding and embrace the reality that God's ways are higher than ours (Isaiah 55:8-9).

Trusting Through Uncertainty

Life often presents challenges that test our faith and trust in God's plan. In these moments, it can be difficult to see how circumstances align with His promises. However, Scripture provides numerous examples of individuals who trusted in God despite uncertainty or adversity.

Consider the story of Joseph in Genesis 37-50. Betrayed by his brothers and sold into slavery, Joseph endured years of hardship before rising to a position of power in Egypt. Despite his trials, Joseph remained faithful to God and ultimately recognized how his suffering served a greater purpose: *"You intended to harm me, but God intended it for good to accomplish what is now being done, the saving of many lives"* (Genesis 50:20). Joseph's story reminds us that even when we cannot see the full picture, we can trust that God is working behind the scenes for our benefit.

Similarly, Jesus Himself demonstrated perfect trust in the Father's plan during His time on earth. In the Garden of Gethsemane, facing imminent crucifixion, Jesus prayed: *"My Father, if it is possible, may this cup be taken from me. Yet not as I will, but as you will"* (Matthew 26:39). This act of submission underscores the importance of aligning our will with God's—even when it involves personal sacrifice or suffering.

The Role of Faith in Trusting God's Plan

Faith plays a central role in trusting God's plan as our true Father. Hebrews 11 defines faith as *"confidence in what we hope for and assurance about what we do not see"* (Hebrews 11:1). This confidence enables believers to rely on God›s promises even when tangible evidence is lacking.

Abraham's journey exemplifies unwavering faith in God's plan. Called by God to leave his homeland without knowing where he was going (Genesis 12:1-4), Abraham obeyed because he trusted God's guidance. Later, when asked to sacrifice his son Isaac—a direct contradiction to God's earlier promise—Abraham demonstrated remarkable faith by believing that God could raise Isaac from the dead if necessary (Hebrews 11:17-19). Abraham's obedience serves as a powerful example for Christians seeking to trust their heavenly Father's plan.

Practical Steps for Trusting God's Plan

While trusting God's plan can be challenging at times, there are practical steps believers can take to cultivate this trust:

1. **Immerse Yourself in Scripture**
   Regularly reading and meditating on God's Word helps reinforce His promises and character. Passages like Psalm 23 remind us of His guidance and provision as our shepherd.

2. **Pray Without Ceasing**

Prayer fosters intimacy with God and allows us to express our fears or doubts while seeking His wisdom (Philippians 4:6-7).

3. **Surround Yourself with Fellow Believers**
   Fellowship with other Christians provides encouragement during difficult seasons (Hebrews 10:24-25).

4. **Reflect on Past Faithfulness**
   Remembering instances where God has been faithful strengthens our confidence in His future plans.

5. **Surrender Control**
   Acknowledge areas where you may be clinging too tightly to your own desires or expectations—and release them into God's hands.

Conclusion

Trusting in God's plan requires humility—a recognition that He knows what is best for us better than we do ourselves—and faith rooted firmly in His unchanging nature as a loving Father who desires only good things for His children (James 1:17). By embracing this perspective through prayerful surrender and reliance on Scripture's truths about Him being sovereign yet personal simultaneously ensures peace amidst life uncertainties.

Chapter 19: How John 3:16 Defines Our Relationship with God

John 3:16 is one of the most well-known and frequently quoted verses in the Bible. It states, "For God so loved the world that He gave His only begotten Son, that whoever believes in Him should not perish but have everlasting life." This single verse encapsulates the essence of God's love for humanity and serves as a cornerstone for understanding our relationship with Him. In this chapter, we will explore how John 3:16 defines our connection to God as our Father, emphasizing His love, sacrifice, and promise of eternal life.

The Foundation of God's Love

The opening words of John 3:16—"For God so loved the world"—immediately establish the depth and universality of God's love. Unlike human love, which can be conditional or limited, God's love is boundless and extends to all people regardless of their background, sins, or shortcomings. This divine love is not merely an abstract concept; it is active and demonstrated through tangible actions.

God's love is foundational to our relationship with Him because it reveals His character as a loving Father who desires a personal connection with each of His children. In earthly terms, a father's love provides security, guidance, and care. Similarly, God's love assures us that we are valued and cherished beyond measure. This assurance forms the basis of our identity as His children.

The Ultimate Sacrifice

The phrase "He gave His only begotten Son" highlights the sacrificial nature of God's love. By sending Jesus Christ to die on the cross for our sins, God made the ultimate sacrifice to reconcile humanity to Himself. This act demonstrates that God's fatherly care goes beyond mere provision or protection; it involves selflessness and a willingness to endure pain for the sake of His children.

In human relationships, a father's sacrifices often reflect his commitment to his family's well-being. Likewise, God's sacrifice through Jesus underscores His commitment to restoring broken relationships with humanity. It also sets an example for believers to emulate in their own lives by practicing selflessness and prioritizing others' needs over their own.

Faith as the Key to Relationship

The next part of John 3:16—"that whoever believes in Him"—introduces faith as the essential element in establishing a relationship with God. Belief in Jesus Christ is not merely intellectual assent but involves trust, reliance, and surrender. Through faith, we acknowledge God as our Father and accept His authority over our lives.

Faith also transforms our perspective on life by aligning our priorities with God's will. As children of God, we are called to live in obedience to His commandments and reflect His character in our interactions with others. This transformation is evidence of a genuine relationship with God rooted in faith.

The Promise of Eternal Life

The final portion of John 3:16—"should not perish but have everlasting life"—offers hope and assurance to believers. Eternal life is more than just an unending existence; it signifies a restored relationship with God that begins in this life and continues into eternity. This promise reflects God's desire for an intimate and enduring connection with His children.

Eternal life also redefines how we view earthly struggles and challenges. As children of God, we can face difficulties with confidence knowing that they are temporary compared to the eternal joy awaiting us in heaven. This perspective encourages us to remain steadfast in our faith and trust in God's plan for our lives.

Living as Children of God

John 3:16 calls us not only to believe but also to live as children of God who embody His love and grace. This involves sharing the message of salvation with others so they too can experience the transformative power of God's fatherly care. It also requires us to cultivate qualities such as humility, forgiveness, and compassion that reflect God's character.

By embracing our identity as children of God defined by

John 3:16, we fulfill our purpose as ambassadors for Christ (2 Corinthians 5:20). Our lives become testimonies to the reality of God's love and serve as invitations for others to join His family.

Conclusion

John 3:16 defines our relationship with God by revealing Him as a loving Father who sacrifices for His children, invites them into a relationship through faith in Jesus Christ, and promises eternal life. This verse encapsulates the heart of Christianity—the good news that we are deeply loved by a perfect Father who desires an everlasting connection with us.

As we meditate on this profound truth, let us respond by living lives that honor God's fatherly care while extending His love to those around us. In doing so, we fulfill our calling as children of truth who reflect their Heavenly Father's glory.

Chapter 20: Proverbs' Wisdom on Parenting and Spiritual Growth

The Book of Proverbs, often referred to as the "book of wisdom," is a treasure trove of practical guidance for living a life that honors God. It provides profound insights into parenting, spiritual growth, and the relationship between discipline and wisdom. In this chapter, we will explore how Proverbs sheds light on God's role as our ultimate Father and how its teachings can guide us in understanding spiritual growth and godly parenting.

The Foundation of Wisdom: Reverence for God

Proverbs 1:7 declares, "The fear of the Lord is the beginning of knowledge; fools despise wisdom and instruction." This verse sets the tone for understanding spiritual growth. True wisdom begins with reverence for God—a deep respect and awe for His authority, power, and love. As children of God, our spiritual journey starts when we recognize Him as our ultimate Father and submit to His guidance.

In parenting, this principle translates into teaching children to honor God above all else. Parents are called to model reverence for God in their own lives, demonstrating what it means to live under His authority. By doing so, they lay a foundation for their children to grow in wisdom and faith.

Discipline as an Expression of Love

One of the recurring themes in Proverbs is the importance of discipline. Proverbs 13:24 states, "Whoever spares the rod hates his son, but he who loves him is diligent to discipline him." While this verse has been widely debated regarding its interpretation, its core message emphasizes that discipline is an act of love. Just as earthly parents discipline their children out of love and concern for their well-being, God disciplines His children to guide them toward righteousness.

Hebrews 12:6 echoes this sentiment: "For the Lord disciplines the one He loves, and chastises every son whom He receives." Spiritual growth often involves correction from God—whether through conviction by the Holy Spirit or lessons learned through life's challenges. Embracing God's discipline requires humility and trust in His perfect plan.

The Contrast Between Wisdom and Foolishness

Proverbs frequently contrasts wise individuals with fools. For example:

- **Proverbs 15:5:** "A fool despises his father's instruction, but whoever heeds reproof is prudent."

- **Proverbs 12:15:** "The way of a fool is right in his own eyes, but a wise man listens to advice."

These verses highlight the importance of being teachable—a quality essential for both spiritual growth and effective parenting. Wise individuals embrace correction and seek counsel from others (and ultimately from God), while fools reject instruction and rely solely on their own understanding.

As children of God, we are called to adopt an attitude of humility and openness to His guidance. Similarly, parents must cultivate an environment where their children feel safe receiving correction without fear or resentment.

Passing Down Wisdom Through Generations

Proverbs 22:6 offers timeless advice on parenting: "Train up a child in the way he should go; even when he is old he will not depart from it." This verse underscores the long-term impact of instilling godly values in children from an early age. Parents have a unique opportunity—and responsibility—to shape their children's character by teaching them biblical principles.

However, this verse also serves as a reminder that spiritual growth is ultimately a personal journey between each individual and God. While parents can provide guidance and support, they cannot force their children to follow Christ; that decision lies with each person's heart.

Humility Before God's Word

Another key aspect emphasized throughout Proverbs is humility before God's Word:

- **Proverbs 3:5-6:** "Trust in the Lord with all your heart, and do not lean on your own understanding. In all your ways acknowledge Him, and He will make straight your paths."

- **Proverbs 16:9:** "The heart of man plans his way, but the Lord establishes his steps."

These verses remind us that true wisdom comes from trusting God's plan rather than relying solely on human reasoning or effort. Spiritual growth involves surrendering control over our lives to Him—a lesson that applies equally well within families striving toward unity under Christ's lordship.

Practical Applications for Today

1. **For Parents:**

   - Model reverence for God through daily prayer/ devotions.

   - Use discipline as an opportunity not only for correction but also discipleship.

   - Encourage open communication about faith struggles/questions without judgment.

2. **For Believers Seeking Growth:** - Regularly study Scripture (especially books like Psalms/Proverbial texts). - Pray specifically asking Holy Spirit reveal areas needing refinement. - Surround yourself w/wise mentors/accountability partners in the church community.

By applying these principles gleaned directly inspired biblical truths found within proverbs believers alike deepen relationship heavenly father simultaneously equipping next generation faithfully walk truth righteousness.

In conclusion, the wisdom found in Proverbs serves as a timeless guide for both parenting and spiritual growth, emphasizing the importance of discipline, humility, and a teachable spirit. Proverbs 15:5 reminds us that rejecting correction is the mark of folly, while embracing reproof demonstrates wisdom and maturity. This principle applies not only to earthly parenting but also to our relationship with God as our ultimate Father. Just as a loving parent disciplines their child for their benefit, God's corrections are acts of love designed to shape us into His image and lead us toward righteousness.

By aligning ourselves with the truths of Proverbs, we learn to value instruction and correction as tools for growth rather than burdens. This perspective fosters a deeper connection with God, allowing us to trust His guidance even when it challenges our comfort or understanding. As children of the Heavenly Father, we are called to reflect His character by living lives marked by humility, obedience, and a willingness to grow through His Word.

Ultimately, Proverbs teaches us that spiritual growth is not a passive process but an active journey requiring submission to God's authority and an open heart ready to receive His wisdom. By embracing this path, we not only strengthen our relationship with Him but also become better equipped to guide others—whether as parents or spiritual mentors—toward the truth of His eternal love and purpose. Let us therefore commit ourselves to living out these principles daily, trusting that our Heavenly Father's wisdom will lead us into abundant life both now and forevermore.

Chapter 21: Foolishness vs. Prudence: Choosing Your Spiritual Pathway

The Bible consistently contrasts the paths of foolishness and prudence, urging believers to choose wisely in their spiritual journey. This chapter delves into the biblical principles that define these two pathways, examining how they shape our relationship with God as our Heavenly Father. By understanding the characteristics of foolishness and prudence, we can better align ourselves with God's will and live as His children.

The Biblical Definition of Foolishness

Foolishness, as described in scripture, is not merely a lack of intelligence but a rejection of wisdom and divine instruction. Proverbs 1:7 states, "The fear of the Lord is the beginning of knowledge; fools despise wisdom and instruction." This verse highlights that foolishness stems from a heart that resists God's guidance and chooses self-reliance over submission to His authority.

In Proverbs 15:5, we read, "A fool spurns a parent's discipline, but whoever heeds correction shows prudence." Here, the Bible draws a direct connection between rejecting correction and living foolishly. Just as earthly parents discipline their children out of love, God disciplines us for our benefit (Hebrews 12:6). To reject His discipline is to walk in foolishness, distancing ourselves from His fatherly care.

The Hallmarks of Prudence

Prudence, on the other hand, is characterized by humility, teachability, and a deep reverence for God. A prudent person seeks wisdom and applies it to their life decisions. Proverbs 14:8 says, "The wisdom of the prudent is to give thought to their ways, but the folly of fools is deception." Prudence involves careful consideration of one's actions in light of God's Word.

Jesus Himself exemplified prudence through His obedience to the Father. In John 5:19-20, He said, "Very truly I tell you, the Son can do nothing by himself; he can do only what he sees his Father doing." As followers of Christ, we are called to emulate this dependence on God's guidance.

The Consequences of Each Pathway

The Bible warns that choosing foolishness leads to destruction. Proverbs 14:12 cautions, "There is a way that appears to be right, but in the end it leads to death." This verse underscores the deceptive nature of foolishness—it may seem appealing or logical at first glance but ultimately results in spiritual ruin.

Conversely, prudence brings life and peace. Proverbs 3:5-6 encourages us to "Trust in the Lord with all your heart and lean not on your own understanding; in all your ways submit to him, and he will make your paths straight." By trusting God and seeking His wisdom, we align ourselves with His perfect plan for our lives.

Practical Steps for Choosing Prudence

1. **Seek God's Wisdom Through Scripture**
   Regular study of the Bible equips us with divine wisdom. Psalm 119:105 declares, "Your word is a lamp for my feet, a light on my path." Immersing ourselves in God's Word helps us discern between foolishness and prudence.

2. **Embrace Correction**
   Accepting reproof from God or godly mentors demonstrates humility and a desire for growth. Proverbs 12:1 states bluntly, "Whoever loves discipline loves knowledge, but whoever hates correction is stupid."

3. **Cultivate a Prayerful Life**
   Prayer fosters intimacy with God and opens our hearts to His guidance. James 1:5 assures us that if we lack wisdom, we should ask God who gives generously without finding fault.

4. **Surround Yourself With Wise Counsel**
   Proverbs 13:20 advises us to "Walk with the wise and become wise; for a companion of fools suffers harm." Associating with spiritually mature individuals encourages prudent decision-making.

5. **Reflect on Your Choices**
   Take time to evaluate whether your actions align with biblical principles. Lamentations 3:40 urges us to "examine our ways and test them."

Living as Children of Truth

Choosing prudence over foolishness reflects our identity as children of truth under God's fatherly care. It requires daily surrender to His will and an ongoing commitment to grow in faith and understanding. As Apostle Bill Amor emphasizes throughout *Who Is My Father?*, our response to divine instruction shapes not only our spiritual identity but also our eternal destiny.

By walking in prudence rather than foolishness, we honor God as our ultimate Father and demonstrate our trust in His perfect wisdom. Let us strive each day to choose wisely—embracing correction when needed—and live lives that glorify Him.

Chapter 22: The Importance of Faith in Becoming Children of Truth

Faith is the cornerstone of the Christian life, serving as the foundation upon which our relationship with God is built. In this chapter, we will explore how faith plays a critical role in transforming believers into "Children of Truth." Drawing from key biblical passages and theological insights, we will examine the nature of faith, its relationship to truth, and how it enables us to live under God's fatherly care.

Understanding Faith as a Gift from God

Faith is not merely an intellectual assent or emotional response; it is a divine gift bestowed by God. Ephesians 2:8-9 states, "For by grace you have been saved through faith. And this is not your own doing; it is the gift of God, not a result of works, so that no one may boast." This passage underscores that faith originates from God's grace and cannot be earned through human effort. It is through this gift that we are able to believe in Jesus Christ as our Savior and accept the truth of God's Word.

Faith enables us to recognize God as our ultimate Father and align ourselves with His truth. Without faith, it is impossible to please God (Hebrews 11:6), for faith serves as the bridge that connects us to Him. Through faith, we acknowledge His sovereignty, trust in His promises, and submit to His authority.

Faith and Truth: An Inseparable Connection

The Bible repeatedly emphasizes the inseparable connection between faith and truth. Jesus declared in John 14:6, "I am the way, and the truth, and the life. No one comes to the Father except through me." To have faith in Jesus is to embrace Him as the embodiment of truth. This means rejecting falsehoods and lies that lead us away from God.

In John 8:31-32, Jesus said to His disciples, "If you abide in my word, you are truly my disciples, and you will know the truth, and the truth will set you free." Faith involves abiding in God's Word—studying it, meditating on it, and living according to its teachings. As we grow in our understanding of Scripture, our faith deepens, enabling us to discern truth from error.

Living as Children of Truth Through Faith

Becoming children of truth requires more than mere belief; it demands a life transformed by faith. James 2:17 reminds us that "faith by itself, if it does not have works, is dead." Genuine faith manifests itself in actions that reflect God's character and align with His will.

One way we live out our faith is by embracing correction and reproof from God's Word. Proverbs 15:5 states, "A fool despises his father's instruction, but whoever heeds reproof is prudent." As children of truth, we must humbly accept God's discipline and allow it to shape us into His likeness.

Another aspect of living as children of truth is demonstrating love for others. Galatians 5:6 teaches that "faith working through love" is what truly matters in Christ Jesus. Our faith compels us to love our neighbors selflessly and sacrificial-ly—a reflection of God's love for us.

Overcoming Doubt Through Faith

Doubt can be a significant obstacle on our journey toward becoming children of truth. However, Scripture provides numerous examples of individuals who overcame doubt through faith. Consider Thomas (often called "Doubting Thomas"), who initially refused to believe in Jesus' resurrec-tion until he saw physical evidence (John 20:24-29). When confronted with the risen Christ, Thomas exclaimed, "My Lord and my God!" Jesus responded by commending those who believe without seeing.

This account reminds us that while doubts may arise at times, they should drive us closer to God rather than away from Him. By seeking Him earnestly through prayer and Scripture study during moments of uncertainty or confu-sion about spiritual matters or life's challenges overall -we strengthen both trust & reliance upon His guidance ultimate-ly leading towards greater clarity regarding purpose/direc-tion moving forward!

Conclusion

Faith serves as both foundation & catalyst enabling believers' transformation into Children aligned w/Truth under Heavenly Father's care! It empowers recognition/acceptance Sovereignty/trustworthiness Promises alongside submission Authority ultimately resulting deeper understanding/ discernment between right/wrong paths chosen throughout lifetime journey ahead!

Chapter 23: Evaluating Loyalties Through Scripture-Based Reflection

In the journey of faith, one of the most critical aspects of spiritual growth is the evaluation of our loyalties. As believers, we are called to align our hearts, minds, and actions with God's truth as revealed in Scripture. This chapter delves into the importance of examining where our ultimate allegiance lies and how Scripture serves as the guiding standard for this reflection.

The Call to Evaluate Loyalties

The Bible repeatedly emphasizes the need for believers to assess their loyalties. In Matthew 6:24, Jesus states, "No one can serve two masters; either you will hate the one and love the other, or you will be devoted to the one and despise the other." This verse underscores a fundamental principle: divided loyalty is incompatible with true discipleship. Our devotion must be singularly focused on God as our ultimate authority.

Similarly, Joshua 24:15 challenges us with these words: "Choose this day whom you will serve." This call to decision-making highlights that loyalty is not merely a passive state but an active choice that requires intentionality and commitment.

The Role of Scripture in Evaluating Loyalties

Scripture serves as both a mirror and a compass in evaluating our loyalties. Hebrews 4:12 describes God's Word as "living and active, sharper than any double-edged sword," capable of discerning "the thoughts and intentions of the heart." Through prayerful study of Scripture, we can uncover areas where our loyalties may have shifted away from God.

For instance, Proverbs 3:5-6 instructs us to "trust in the Lord with all your heart and lean not on your own understanding; in all your ways submit to him, and he will make your paths straight." This passage reminds us that misplaced trust—whether in ourselves, others, or material possessions—can lead us astray. By aligning our decisions with biblical principles, we reaffirm our loyalty to God.

Identifying Competing Loyalties

One of the challenges in evaluating loyalties is recognizing competing influences that vie for our attention and devotion. These may include:

1. **Materialism:** The pursuit of wealth or possessions can subtly replace God as our primary focus (Matthew 6:19-21).

2. **Relationships:** While relationships are important, they should never take precedence over our relationship with God (Luke 14:26).

3. **Cultural Norms**: Societal values often conflict with

biblical teachings, requiring discernment to remain faithful (Romans 12:2).

By identifying these competing influences through scriptural reflection, we can address them proactively and realign ourselves with God's will.

Practical Steps for Scripture-Based Reflection

To effectively evaluate loyalties through Scripture-based reflection, consider these practical steps:

1. **Daily Devotionals:** Set aside time each day to read and meditate on God's Word.

2. **Prayerful Examination:** Ask God to reveal areas where your loyalties may be divided.

3. **Accountability Partners**: Share your reflections with trusted fellow believers who can provide encouragement and guidance.

4. **Journaling:** Document insights from your study of Scripture and how they apply to your life.

5. **Obedience:** Act on what you learn by making changes that reflect greater alignment with biblical principles.

The Rewards of Undivided Loyalty

When we commit ourselves fully to God, we experience

profound spiritual rewards. Psalm 37:4 promises that those who delight themselves in the Lord will receive "the desires of [their] heart." This does not mean that all earthly desires will be fulfilled but rather that our desires will become aligned with God's purposes.

Moreover, undivided loyalty fosters peace and confidence in times of uncertainty. Isaiah 26:3 declares, "You will keep in perfect peace those whose minds are steadfast because they trust in you."

Conclusion

Evaluating loyalties through Scripture-based reflection is an ongoing process essential for spiritual maturity. By using God's Word as our standard, we can identify areas where our devotion has wavered and take steps toward realignment. In doing so, we honor God as our ultimate Father and strengthen our identity as His children.

Chapter 24: Living Out the Truth as Sons and Daughters of God

Living out the truth as sons and daughters of God is a profound calling that requires both understanding and application of biblical principles in every aspect of life. This chapter delves into what it means to embody the identity of being God's children, exploring how believers can align their lives with His truth, reflect His character, and fulfill their divine purpose.

Understanding Our Identity in Christ

The foundation for living out the truth begins with understanding our identity in Christ. John 1:12 states, "Yet to all who did receive him, to those who believed in his name, he gave the right to become children of God." This verse underscores that becoming a child of God is not based on human effort or merit but on receiving Jesus Christ through faith. As sons and daughters of God, believers are adopted into His family (Romans 8:15), gaining access to His love, guidance, and eternal inheritance.

This identity is transformative. It redefines how we view ourselves and others. No longer are we defined by worldly standards or past mistakes; instead, we are seen as beloved children of a perfect Father. This realization should inspire humility, gratitude, and a commitment to live according to God's will.

Walking in Truth and Righteousness

To live out the truth as God's children means walking in truth and righteousness. Ephesians 5:1-2 exhorts believers to "follow God's example, therefore, as dearly loved children and walk in the way of love, just as Christ loved us." Walking in truth involves aligning our thoughts, words, and actions with God's Word. It requires rejecting falsehoods and embracing honesty, integrity, and moral uprightness.

Proverbs 3:5-6 provides practical guidance for this journey: "Trust in the Lord with all your heart and lean not on your own understanding; in all your ways submit to him, and he will make your paths straight." Trusting God means relying on His wisdom rather than our limited perspective. Submitting to Him involves seeking His guidance through prayer and scripture study while being obedient to His commands.

Reflecting the Father's Character

As children of God, we are called to reflect His character in our interactions with others. Matthew 5:16 encourages us to let our light shine before others so that they may see our good deeds and glorify our Father in heaven. This light is not self-generated but flows from a close relationship with God.

Reflecting God's character includes demonstrating love (1 Corinthians 13), showing compassion (Colossians 3:12), extending forgiveness (Ephesians 4:32), pursuing justice (Micah 6:8), and practicing humility (Philippians 2:3). These qualities set believers apart from the world and serve as a testimony to God's transformative power.

Embracing Discipline as Sons and Daughters

Hebrews 12:6 reminds us that "the Lord disciplines the one he loves." Discipline is an essential aspect of living out the truth because it shapes us into Christlikeness. While discipline may be uncomfortable at times, it is evidence of God's love and commitment to our growth.

Embracing discipline involves accepting correction with humility (Proverbs 15:5) and allowing it to refine our character. It also means being proactive in cultivating spiritual disciplines such as prayer, fasting, worship, fellowship with other believers, and studying scripture.

Living Missionally as Children of God

Finally, living out the truth entails fulfilling our mission as ambassadors for Christ (2 Corinthians 5:20). As sons and daughters of God, we are entrusted with sharing the gospel message with others so that they too may experience reconciliation with Him.

This mission requires boldness (Acts 4:29), perseverance (Galatians 6:9), sensitivity to the Holy Spirit's leading (John 16:13), and a heart for service (Matthew 20:28). Whether through acts of kindness or verbal proclamation of the gospel message—every believer has a role in advancing God's kingdom on earth.

Conclusion

Living out the truth as sons and daughters of God is both a privilege and responsibility. It begins with understanding our identity in Christ but extends into every area of life— our thoughts must align with His Word; our actions should reflect His character; our hearts need openness toward correction; finally—we must actively participate within His mission field daily!

By doing so faithfully—we honor Him fully—as true heirs destined eternally alongside Him forevermore!

Chapter 25: Who is My Father? Answering Life's Most Profound Question

The question "Who is my Father?" is one of the most profound and spiritually significant inquiries a person can ask. It transcends biological relationships, cultural norms, and societal expectations, delving into the very core of our existence and identity. In this final chapter, we will explore the ultimate answer to this question through the lens of scripture, theology, and personal reflection. By understanding God as our true Father, we uncover not only His divine nature but also our purpose as His children.

The Biblical Foundation

The Bible consistently portrays God as the ultimate Father—loving, just, merciful, and sovereign. This concept is rooted in key scriptures such as John 3:16, Matthew 23:9, and Proverbs 15:5. These verses collectively reveal God's character and His relationship with humanity:

- **John 3:16** emphasizes God›s immense love for the world, demonstrated by the sacrifice of His only Son so that believers may have eternal life. This act of love establishes God as a Father who desires an intimate relationship with His children.

- **Matthew 23:9** instructs believers not to call anyone on earth their spiritual father because God alone holds that position. This verse underscores God›s unique authority and role in guiding His people.

- **Proverbs 15:5** contrasts the attitudes of fools who reject correction with wise individuals who embrace reproof. This wisdom highlights God›s fatherly discipline as an expression of His care for us.

These scriptures form the foundation for understanding God as our true Father—a relationship that defines our spiritual identity and shapes our lives.

The Nature of Our Heavenly Father

God's nature as a Father is multifaceted. He is both transcendent and immanent—beyond human comprehension yet intimately involved in our lives. The following attributes illustrate His fatherly character:

1. **Unconditional Love:** Unlike earthly fathers whose love may be conditional or flawed, God›s love is perfect and unchanging (Romans 8:38-39). He loves us not because of what we do but because of who He is.

2. **Discipline and Guidance:** As Proverbs 3:11-12 states, "My son, do not despise the Lord's discipline...because the Lord disciplines those he loves." God's correction is always aimed at our growth and well-being.

3. **Provider:** God meets all our needs according to His riches in glory (Philippians 4:19). He provides not only material blessings but also spiritual nourishment through His Word.

4. **Protector:** Psalm 91 describes God as a refuge and fortress for those who trust in Him. He shields us from harm and delivers us from evil.

5. **Faithful Promise-Keeper:** Every promise God makes is fulfilled (Numbers 23:19). We can trust Him completely because He never fails.

Our Identity as Children of God

Understanding God as our Father transforms how we see ourselves and live our lives. When we accept Jesus Christ as Lord and Savior, we are adopted into God's family (Ephesians 1:5). This adoption grants us several privileges:

- **A New Identity:** We are no longer defined by sin or worldly standards but by our status as children of God (2 Corinthians 5:17).

- **An Eternal Inheritance:** As heirs with Christ, we share in the riches of God›s kingdom (Romans 8:17).

- **Access to the Father:** Through prayer, we can approach God boldly and confidently (Hebrews 4:16).

- **A Purposeful Life:** Our calling is to glorify God by reflecting His love to others (Matthew 5:16).

Living as children of God requires humility, obedience, and faithfulness. It means aligning our thoughts, words, and actions with His will.

Contrasting Earthly Fathers with Our Heavenly Father

While earthly fathers play an important role in shaping their children's lives, they are imperfect reflections of God's fatherhood. Some may struggle with absenteeism or fail to provide adequate love and support due to their own limitations or brokenness.

In contrast:

- God's presence is constant; He will never leave nor forsake us (Deuteronomy 31:6).

- His wisdom surpasses human understanding; He knows what is best for us even when we do not (Isaiah 55:8-9).

- His forgiveness has no bounds; He welcomes prodigal sons and daughters back into His arms without hesitation (Luke 15:11-32).

Recognizing these differences helps us place ultimate trust in God rather than relying solely on human relationships.

Conclusion:

In answering the question, "Who is my Father?" we are drawn to the ultimate truth that transcends human understanding and earthly relationships. God, as revealed through His Word, stands as the eternal and unchanging Father of all creation. He is not only the Creator but also the

Redeemer, who through Jesus Christ has made a way for humanity to be reconciled to Him. This profound relationship with God as our Father is not based on merit or works but on His grace and love, as demonstrated in John 3:16.

Recognizing God as our Father reshapes our identity and purpose. It calls us to live as children of truth, embracing His correction, guidance, and love with humility and faith. As Proverbs 15:5 reminds us, wisdom comes from accepting reproof and aligning ourselves with His divine will. Furthermore, Matthew 23:9 challenges us to place our ultimate loyalty in God alone, acknowledging Him as the supreme authority over every aspect of our lives.

The journey of understanding who our true Father is leads us to a deeper sense of belonging and security in His promises. It equips us to navigate life's uncertainties with confidence in His sovereignty and eternal plan. By living under His fatherly care, we find rest for our souls (Matthew 11:28-30) and assurance of an eternal inheritance (Romans 8:17).

Ultimately, answering this profound question requires a personal response—choosing to accept God's invitation to become His child through faith in Jesus Christ. In doing so, we not only discover who our true Father is but also embrace the fullness of life He offers now and forevermore. Let this truth guide your heart and mind as you walk daily in the light of His love.

Conclusion: Embracing God as Our True Father

In the journey through this book, we have explored the profound and transformative truth of God as our ultimate Father. From the foundational scripture of John 3:16, which reveals His immense love for humanity and His gift of eternal life through Jesus Christ, to the teachings of Matthew 23:9 that call us to recognize God alone as our spiritual authority, we have seen how these truths shape our identity as His children. Proverbs 15:5 has further illuminated the importance of humility and a willingness to embrace correction, hallmarks of those who live under God's fatherly care.

Understanding God as our Father is not merely a theological concept; it is an invitation to a deeply personal relationship with Him. This relationship calls us to align ourselves with truth and righteousness, rejecting the lies and deceptions that seek to pull us away from His love. It challenges us to evaluate our loyalties, prioritize divine instruction over earthly influences, and trust in His sovereignty over all aspects of our lives.

As children of God, we are called to live in alignment with His will, reflecting His love and grace in our interactions with others. This requires humility, faith, and a commitment to walking in truth. It also involves embracing discipline and correction as expressions of His care for us, knowing that He desires what is best for our growth and ultimate good.

The contrast between living as "Children of Truth" versus following lies underscores the critical choice each person must make. Will we accept God's gift of eternal life through Jesus Christ and live under His guidance as our loving Father? Or will we reject His truth and follow paths that lead away from Him? The answer to this question shapes not only our spiritual identity but also our eternal destiny.

As you close this book, may you be encouraged to deepen your relationship with God as your true Father. Seek Him daily through prayer, study His Word diligently, and allow His Spirit to guide you in all things. Remember that you are loved beyond measure by the Creator of the universe—a Father who knows you intimately, cares for you deeply, and desires nothing less than your ultimate joy and fulfillment in Him.

May your life be a testament to the transformative power of living as a child of God—walking in truth, embracing righteousness, and shining His light into a world desperately in need of hope. Let this understanding propel you forward into a life marked by faithfulness, obedience, and unwavering trust in your Heavenly Father.

In closing, remember these words from Romans 8:15-16: "For you did not receive a spirit that makes you a slave again to fear; but you received the Spirit of sonship. And by him we cry, 'Abba, Father.' The Spirit himself testifies with our spirit that we are God's children." May this truth anchor your heart always.

Heavenly Father,

We come before You with hearts full of gratitude and reverence, acknowledging You as the one true Father of all who are born again through faith in Jesus Christ. You are the Alpha and the Omega, the Creator of heaven and earth, the Giver of life, and the Sustainer of our souls. We thank You for Your immeasurable love that was so perfectly demonstrated in John 3:16—that You gave Your only begotten Son so that we might have eternal life. What a privilege it is to be called Your children, adopted into Your family through the Spirit of truth.

Lord, we recognize that as born-again believers, we are orphans in this world when it comes to earthly fathers. No matter how godly or loving our earthly fathers may be, they cannot stand beside us when we meet Jesus face-to-face. It is only by Your grace and mercy that we can approach Your throne with confidence. Help us to fully embrace our identity as sons and daughters of God Almighty, knowing that our ultimate allegiance is to You alone.

Father, we live in a world that lies in wickedness—a world filled with deception, darkness, and rebellion against Your truth. Yet You have called us out of this darkness into Your marvelous light. Strengthen us to walk as children of truth, reflecting Your righteousness and love in every aspect of our lives. Teach us to reject the lies of this world and cling steadfastly to Your Word, which is a lamp unto our feet and a light unto our path.

We pray for humility to accept Your correction and reproof as Proverbs 15:5 teaches us. Mold us into wise children who delight in learning from You and growing under Your fatherly care. May we never forget that You discipline those whom You love, shaping us into vessels fit for Your glory.

Lord Jesus, we eagerly await the day when we will see You face-to-face—when all tears will be wiped away, all pain will cease, and we will dwell in perfect communion with You forever. Until that day comes, help us to remain faithful stewards of the gospel message. Empower us by Your Holy Spirit to share the good news with others so they too may come to know You as their Father.

Abba Father, thank You for adopting us into Your family through the blood of Jesus Christ. Thank You for being our refuge, our strength, and our ever-present help in times of trouble. We surrender ourselves completely to You today— our hearts, minds, souls, and bodies—knowing that apart from You we can do nothing.

May this book serve as a beacon of hope for those seeking their true identity in Christ. May it inspire readers to draw closer to You as their heavenly Father and deepen their understanding of what it means to live as children of God.

We give all glory, honor, and praise to You alone—the King eternal, immortal, invisible—the only wise God! In Jesus' mighty name we pray, Amen.

Rev 12:10 And I heard a loud voice saying in heaven, Now is come salvation, and strength, and the kingdom of our God, and the power of his Christ: for the accuser of our brethren is cast down, which accused them before our God day and night.

John 15:4 Abide in me, and I in you. As the branch cannot bear fruit of itself, except it abide in the vine; no more can ye, except ye abide in me.

Rom 8:1 There is therefore now no condemnation to them which are in Christ Jesus, who walk not after the flesh, but after the Spirit.

1 Th 4:11 And that ye study to be quiet,
and to do your own business,
and to work with your own hands,
as we commanded you;

Matt 11:25 At that time Jesus answered and said, I thank thee, O Father, Lord of heaven and earth, because thou hast hid these things from the wise and prudent, and hast revealed them unto babes. 26Even so, Father: for so it seemed good in thy sight. 27All things are delivered unto me of my Father: and no man knoweth the Son, but the Father; neither knoweth any man the Father, save the Son, and he to whomsoever the Son will reveal him.

28Come unto me, all ye that labour and are heavy laden, and I will give you rest. 29Take my yoke upon you, and learn of me; for I am meek and lowly in heart: and ye shall find rest unto your souls. 30For my yoke is easy, and my burden is light.

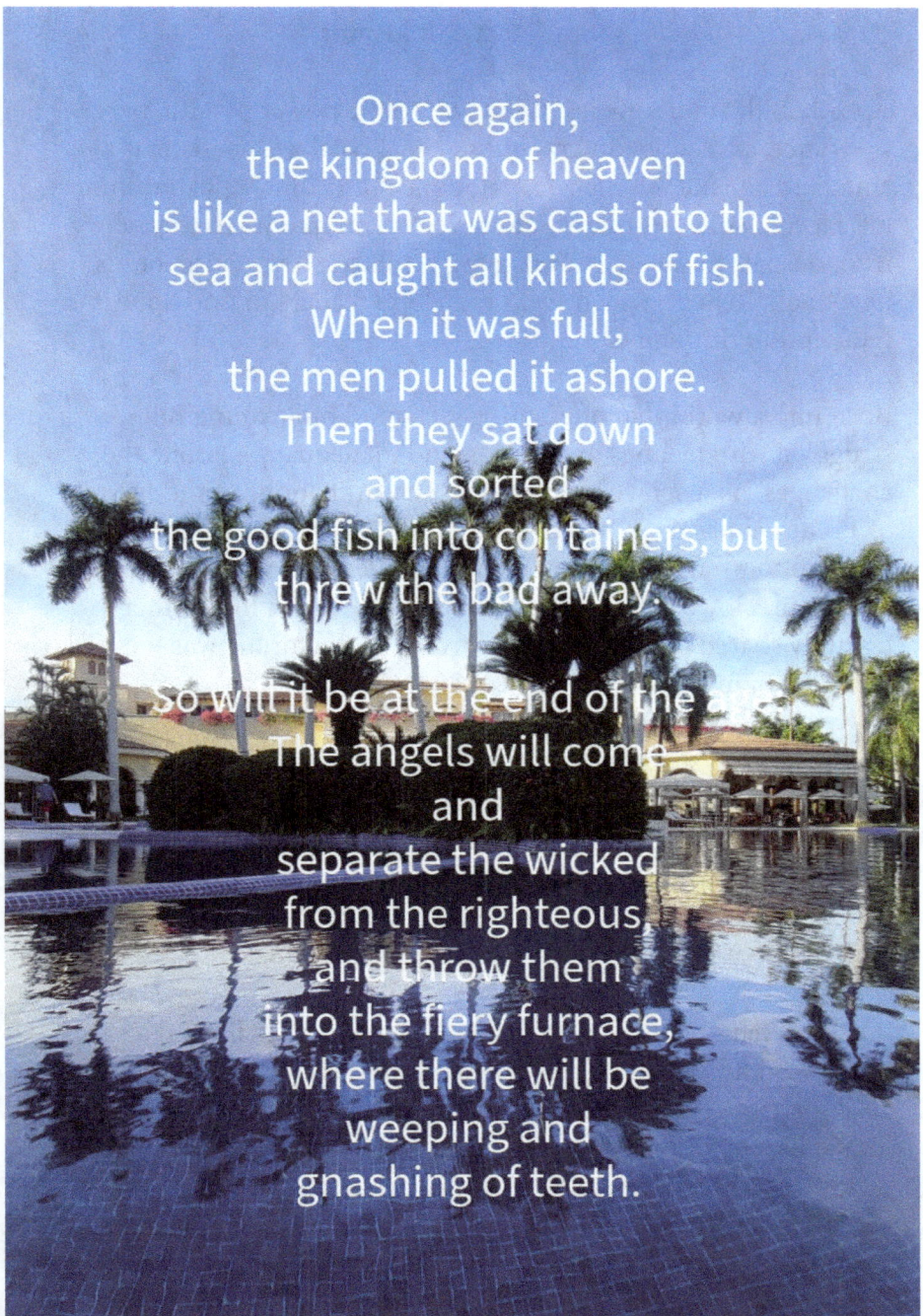

Once again,
the kingdom of heaven
is like a net that was cast into the
sea and caught all kinds of fish.
When it was full,
the men pulled it ashore.
Then they sat down
and sorted
the good fish into containers, but
threw the bad away.

So will it be at the end of the age.
The angels will come
and
separate the wicked
from the righteous,
and throw them
into the fiery furnace,
where there will be
weeping and
gnashing of teeth.

About Apostle Bill Amor

Apostle Bill Amor's life is a testament to the power of faith, perseverance, and divine intervention. Diagnosed with autism as a child and considered high-functioning as an adult, Apostle Amor has faced challenges that would have broken many. His journey from despair to spiritual awakening forms the foundation of his new book, Repent, which seeks to inspire readers to find hope and redemption through God.

Born into a world that often misunderstood him, young Bill struggled with feelings of isolation and inadequacy. Despite these challenges, he displayed remarkable determination. At the age of 12, he achieved a significant milestone by winning a reading competition—an accomplishment that filled him with pride and optimism. However, this joy was short-lived when his mother tearfully shared devastating news from the doctor: he was not expected to live beyond the age of 28 to 32.

This revelation shattered his world. Overwhelmed by fear and hopelessness, Bill sought solace in his best friend John Straw, only to discover that John had been taken away by his brother Andy. Feeling abandoned and consumed by anger, he fled into the woods near his home. It was there, amidst the trees and shadows of doubt, that he cried out to God in desperation.

Bill's life changed forever on that fateful day. As he climbed a steep hill toward his neighbor's house, he encountered what can only be described as a divine vision: Jesus Christ Himself appeared before him at the top of the hill near a chain-link fence. The image was vivid—Jesus stood before him with pockmarks where His beard had been removed and glistening divots on His cheeks and chin. He did not resemble traditional depictions; instead, He appeared timeless yet distinct from modern trends.

This miraculous encounter marked the beginning of Apostle Amor's transformation. From a young boy who felt lost and unworthy, he grew into a man devoted to spreading God's message of love and repentance. Through trials and tribulations—including struggles with literacy—he found strength in faith and discovered his purpose as an apostle.

In Repent, Apostle Bill Amor shares his deeply personal story alongside powerful lessons about redemption, forgiveness, and unwavering trust in God's plan. His journey serves as an inspiration for anyone grappling with doubt or seeking meaning in their lives.

Apostle Amor's mission is clear: to guide others toward spiritual healing by sharing his testimony of divine grace. With humility born from hardship and wisdom gained through faith, he invites readers to embark on their own journeys toward repentance and renewal.

Who is My Father?